THE BRITISH WAY TO RECOVERY

HUMPHREY MILFORD
OXFORD UNIVERSITY PRESS
LONDON

THE RYERSON PRESS
TORONTO

THE BRITISH WAY
TO RECOVERY

*PLANS AND POLICIES IN GREAT
BRITAIN, AUSTRALIA, AND CANADA*

✓ ✓ ✓

HERBERT HEATON

PROFESSOR OF ECONOMIC HISTORY
UNIVERSITY OF MINNESOTA

1934
THE UNIVERSITY OF MINNESOTA PRESS
MINNEAPOLIS

COPYRIGHT 1934 BY THE
UNIVERSITY OF MINNESOTA

Published November 19, 1934
Second Printing November 27, 1934

PRINTED IN THE UNITED STATES OF AMERICA

⸗ PREFACE ⸗

THIS LITTLE BOOK IS THE UNEXPECTED OUTCOME OF A luncheon talk given to that lively group, the Students Forum, at the University of Minnesota last spring. I was ordered to describe and analyze, for an audience that was well acquainted with American recovery efforts, the policies pursued by Great Britain in face of depression and crisis. I was then asked to turn the talk into a pamphlet, and then to expand the pamphlet into a book, adding some account of Canadian and Australian developments.

The task promised to be a light summer exercise, but has not kept its promise. It is far too big to be covered in one book, and it is one that cannot be done properly for some time to come. Years must pass before we can measure the effect of many plans and policies in promoting or delaying recovery, and in giving new slants and direction to the economic development and character of the countries concerned. A deep long depression, like a long war, leaves permanent marks, or scars, on economic and political life, and policies that are adopted under the stress of adversity may persist long after the dark days have passed. Britain, Canada, and Australia are emerging from the depression with organization and policies very different from those of 1929; but we cannot yet say which of these changes will be permanent.

To Canadian and Australian readers, if there be any, a word of apology is needed for the title of this book.

My only excuses are that the work deals with three parts of the British Commonwealth of Nations, and that the story would have been different in each area if there had been no political connection. But I recognize freely that the two large dominions have pursued paths of their own: that of Australia was in large measure hewn through the bush by her own publicists, both political and academic, while Canada has, since March, 1933, found it increasingly difficult to keep her feet off the tracks made by the trail-blazers of Washington.

The material used in this study has been drawn from various obvious sources. Information collected during a year's residence in England has been supplemented from the *Economist*, the *London Times*, the *Manchester Guardian*, the weeklies, and some official publications. For Australia no better source can be tapped than the articles and books written by that handful of Australian economists whose work in diagnosis and prescription is one of the best pieces of political economy in modern times. Canadian studies are more scanty, and I have had to draw on information collected from the press, from official publications, and from conversations with Canadians during two summers spent in the Dominion. My colleagues, Professor A. L. Burt and Mr. Herbert Tout, and my wife have corrected many errors due to astigmatism, and to them I am grateful; but it is hard to see clearly through the darkness and driving spray of the last four years.

HERBERT HEATON

University of Minnesota
October, 1934

CONTENTS

CHAPTER ONE

THE BRITISH OLD DEAL

EARLY IN AUGUST, 1931, I CALLED IN NEW YORK ON THE secretary of a foundation that had given me a fellowship for a year's research work in England. He was worried by the contents of a cable which had just arrived, for it reported that another fellow, then in Germany, had lost all his money through the collapse of the Darmstadt Bank, and had nothing left for his return ticket. "How are you carrying your money?" I was asked. "Dollars and pounds," I replied, and it was unanimously agreed that I was perfectly safe, for nothing evil could happen to Britain, her banks, or her currency.

Ten days later we landed at Plymouth, in time to watch the worst phase of the economic blizzard sweep away one landmark after another. The Labor government fell, the gold standard ceased to stand. Free trade, the policy that had prevailed for over eighty years, vanished. Every evening we switched on the radio for the six o'clock "First News Bulletin," asking "What next?" and as we looked at the figures of unemployment or of the national deficit we wondered if this was the last twilight of a land that once had been the world's workshop, shipper, and banker.

When we left, a year later, most of our doubts had been dispelled. The country was regaining confidence, had emerged from the darkest hours, and was stepping toward sunlight. The contrast between the two ends of the westward passage was startling, for as we came back to New York, to Detroit, and to Minneapolis we seemed to have passed from hope to despair, from convalescence to creeping paralysis. How well-grounded this impression was, the events of the following winter were to prove. Great Britain went into depression at the same time as did the United States – in the fall of 1929; she reached her crisis eighteen months before America, and had got over it before ours came. Her recovery set in during the summer of 1932, was checked by our breakdown in the winter of 1932–1933, but soon gathered momentum again.

By the middle of 1934 the evidence of recovery was substantial. The number of persons unemployed had fallen from three to two million; the number of people actually employed was as large as on the eve of the depression. In the darkest month one worker out of every four was idle; today it is one out of six, but in the twenties it was one out of ten, and in prosperous pre-war years probably only one out of twenty workers was unemployed.

As men have been called back to work and new workers fresh from school have been absorbed, the volume of industrial production has increased. A Board of Trade index number shows a rise from 97 in 1932 to 118 for the second quarter of 1934. This improvement is widespread. The output of the old staple industries – woolen, machinery, iron, steel, and coal – has expanded somewhat, though that of cotton still languishes. Even the shipyards, which for four years have been silent as graveyards, have begun to resound once more with the noise of riveting machines.

The export of coal and manufactured wares has begun to creep up. But recovery has come chiefly from expansion or revival of the home market, rather than from an influx of orders from overseas. The home market has grown in both meanings of the word "home." In the first place, cheap materials and low interest rates on such long-term loans as mortgages have made possible a great expansion in housebuilding and slum clearance, and produced a veritable building boom. This has increased the demand for materials, and has reacted on other industries. The need for more homes and better homes is so great that saturation point is still far off. In the second place, certain commodities from farm and factory, once largely imported, are now obtained in greater measure from domestic producers. A protective policy and a depreciated pound have given shelter to the local producer; British firms have improved their methods of production or the quality of their product, while American branch factories have been established in increasing numbers to make on the spot wares once drawn from this side of the Atlantic. Recent exhibits in America of British films have shown us how Hollywood's monopoly is being challenged; the supremacy of Detroit has also been disputed, for whereas in 1925 one car out of every four sold in Britain came from North America, in 1933 only one car out of every fifty was imported.

At almost every point on the statistical map the figures for 1934 look healthier. If we turn from the indications of convalescence in private enterprise to public affairs, the outstanding fact has been the declaration by the Chancellor of the Exchequer in April, 1934, that he had a surplus in hand, and was therefore able to reduce certain taxes and restore certain cuts made in 1931 in the salaries of public servants and in payments to the unemployed. This announcement was made at a time when we were all reading a posthumous work by Dickens, and the Chancellor therefore voiced a hope that Great Britain, after spending many years in "Bleak House," could now begin to entertain "Great Expectations."

He might have added that many were still experiencing "Hard Times" and, like Mr. Micawber, waiting for something to turn up. In spite of the substantial recovery which has been made, the country is still far from being "through" her troubles. At best she has moved far enough in the long tunnel to be able to see the tiny spot of light at the far end; but the spot is far off, and, if history repeats itself, there are other tunnels ahead on that track.

These mildly cheerful developments have prompted comparisons with our own recent history. During the boom years of the twenties Englishmen swarmed across the Atlantic to discover the secrets of American prosperity; we now return the compliment by searching for the secrets of British recovery. Conditions have improved on both sides of the ocean. We have had our New Deal, the most ambitious and lavishly financed effort ever made by any country to round the now famous corner. Has Britain had anything comparable, or has she lived up to her reputation for muddling through, stumbling like a shortsighted and not very intelligent man, up to the knees in mud, through a London fog? Has she had any "shots in the arm," any generous "priming of the pump," or did she "let nature take its course"? If she did, would not nature have brought us along the same road to convalescence?

Such questions bubble forth, but behind them is a much more fundamental one. Can government action do much that is positive and constructive to dissipate depression? To that question most politicians would readily answer "Yes," but most economists would be much less certain. Let us analyze political action in dark days. Three R's demand attention — not the three of the little red schoolhouse, but relief, reform, and recovery; and perhaps we should add retribution as a fourth.

Relief of the victims of depression, or of some of them, is generally admitted to be a duty of government, and when the need is great even federal governments must come to the aid of towns and states or provinces. Relief from the menace of starvation, from the claims of the creditor, from the pressure of high costs, and even from the shadow of bankruptcy — the last three years are full of instances in most countries.

Retribution and reform have also occupied our attention, for the strain of depression has torn rents in our economic fabric and pulled aside the veil behind which various forms of original sin and of the acquisitive instinct have sheltered. As defects in our banking, corporation, stock exchange, and other structures have been revealed, and as the list of personal devils has grown longer, we have striven to punish sinners and erect better fences to keep their successors from transgressing. We have burned our fingers, we want the scalps of the men who lit the fire, and we are trying to design effective fireguards. At the same time we are seeking to protect the dependent and the helpless against such exploitation as we now know they suffered in the past, and even the most skeptical seem agreed that attacks on child labor, long hours, and low wages are justified and necessary.

But what of recovery? What can governments do to start or stimulate it? A change of government may have valuable psychological effects if people feel that "something" will now be done, and therefore shed their pessimism. A government may pump some buying power and cheap credit into the community, and if it is able to reduce the rate of interest on long-term loans it may make loan capital cheaper to potential borrowers and thus stimulate enterprise along lines that have been barred by high interest charges. It may start a wave of speculative buying by plans for "monkeying with the currency." It may change and improve the conditions in which private enterprise has to operate by altering its tariff policy, reducing its taxes, amending its laws, adding to the services it renders, or removing some obstacle from the path.

But it cannot get men moving again until they see a prospect of profit ahead, for the profit motive remains the driving force in most economic enterprise. There probably never before was so much idle credit as today, so many business men afraid to borrow, or so many bank managers wondering what to do with the funds in their hands. Governments cannot bring back good prices until the load of commodities that hangs over a market has been removed, and their efforts to prop up prices may even delay recovery.

Government action is often determined by political, or party-political, considerations to win the support, stave off the hostility, or quiet the clamor of some section or group. A step taken to save or stimulate one interest may injure another, rob Peter of much to pay Paul a little; or if both Peter and Paul receive help one effort may cancel the effect of the other. Further, action may be determined by national considerations, yet the economic interests of a large part of the population and the causes of depression may be international. As Mr. Clay puts it, "The tendency of national governments, confronted with a loss of world equilibrium, is to aggravate it by seeking to correct only those effects that are obvious within their own territories."[1] The intensification of economic nationalism since 1929 has been both a result of depression and a cause of the deepening of the disorder. Every government has tried to discourage imports and encourage exports, and the net result has been a further shrinkage of international trade and of those industries which, because of superior resources or equipment, were large exporters. Each country tries to strengthen its weak industries at the expense of the strong ones in other lands; and the other lands retort by hitting its strong industries.

Political effort to stimulate recovery is limited in its effect by the ignorance, or at least the wide differences of opinion, concerning the causes of depression and of

[1] In *The World's Economic Crisis and the Way of Escape* (1932), p. 152.

recovery. The "boom and burst" parts of the business cycle have been studied intensively, yet it would be hard to get agreement among economists concerning the causes of the slump that began in 1929, and scarcely anyone has attempted to study recovery, the forces that set it in motion, or the prerequisites to the operation of those forces. Since that is so, government action must be a leap in the dark; we take such action as is within our national power, as seems likely to have good results, or as is called for by a sufficiently large or vociferous group; but the expected does not always happen, while the unexpected sometimes does.

Finally, when we speak of recovery we must think not merely of recovery *from*, but also of recovery *of*. What do we hope to recover today? The conditions of the twenties? Those conditions rested on great outlays of capital to equip parts of the world with roads, buildings, power plants, electrical appliances and generators, automobiles, rayon, and various other new or old necessaries, comforts, or luxuries. These demands reacted on the producers of raw materials and machines; they gave added work to transportation and multiplied the number of salesmen and providers of service; they called for the mobilization, organization, and export of vast sums of capital, stimulated financial centers, and gave business to the industries that supplied the capital export goods.

If recovery depends on the restoration of the conditions of this great investment boom, all the king's ministers and all the president's men can do little. Foreign investment has become unpopular, and will regain favor only slowly. The task of supplying America and some other countries with their roads, cars, radios, skyscrapers, power plants, and so forth has been almost completed, and no great new demand has yet arisen to take the place of those which were so intense during the twenties. The gradual wearing out of the old equipment and the supplying of some markets which are not yet saturated will give the industries that flourished eight years ago a modest amount of business, but their hectic youth is probably ended, and a new generation is slow in making its appearance.

The part that government can play in recovery is thus limited. In the years ahead we can expect to see a long line of masters' and doctors' theses examining the direct and indirect effect of public efforts to stimulate the current recovery. Many of them will probably show that governments helped here and hindered there; many will be variations on a theme expounded in 1933 by a British economist who said that the business cycle, in its ineffable wisdom, began to move upward in 1932 and since that time has continued to do so, in spite of the fatheadedness of the German government, the pigheadedness of the British government, and the featherheadedness of the American government. If depression had a political cause it might have a political cure, but in so far as its cause was economic its cure must be found in economic rather than political remedies, and since most depressions are the price paid for excesses in production and finance during the preceding boom, no political action can prevent someone from having to pay the price.

The British government, like all others, had to "do something," and has been busy wrestling with the R's.

When we compare its efforts since the crisis of mid-1931 with those of the American administration, we see at once that there were certain things that Britain *could* not do, and many things that she *need* not do. She could not afford to face a series of large deficits in her national accounts, but must try to balance her budget from year to year. She could not increase her national debt seriously by borrowing heavily, for her resources were already mortgaged to the hilt by a dead-weight debt, the cost of past wars. She could not seek to raise prices greatly or quickly, for that would hurt her export trade, raise the cost of living, and flood the country with demands for higher wages. She could not base great hope of recovery on the revival of agriculture. If any such measures might have helped, London's inability to take them, or pin great expectations on them, made her task much more difficult than that of Washington.

On the other hand, Britain's task was easier and lighter in many respects, since there were many things she need not do. The New Deal has attempted relief, retribution, reform, and recovery all at once, and some of its critics have suggested that the first three have impeded the fourth, and taken away with one hand what was given with the other. There is little disinterested opposition to the aim of some of the reforms. But reform and relief have faced the administration with Herculean tasks, called for the erection of emergency machinery to frame and administer the various measures, and, by affecting so many sides of life simultaneously, have stirred up opposition and uncertainty at a score of points.

The British government had no such load to shoulder,

for many of the problems we are now tackling had emerged earlier and had been dealt with in a piecemeal fashion during the last hundred and thirty years. Much of the New Deal was part of Britain's Old Deal.

There was, for example, no need to worry, in the depths of a crisis, with the problem of labor conditions or relationships. The first attempt to deal with child labor was made in 1802, in a small half-hearted way, but in 1833 the matter was taken up more seriously. Bit by bit, as experience and need accumulated, the ban on child labor was spread over the whole industrial and commercial field, and the principle was established that childhood is a period for education and play, not for wage-earning.

There was no need to wrestle with the question of working hours, for here again, during a century and over an ever widening field the state had been limiting hours of labor. Where the state had not done it the trade unions and the enlightened self-interest of some employers had. There was no need to fight the sweating employer over the starvation wages he paid, for the unions had been looking after that matter with increasing success since about 1850, while the state made the protection of notoriously ill-paid occupations one of its duties in 1909.

It was not necessary to help labor to win the right of collective bargaining, for the unions had slowly won that for themselves, while the state had helped to build machinery for mediation, conciliation, or arbitration. In 1928 eight million workers out of fourteen million were working under conditions determined largely by collective bargaining. Where a fundamental issue, such as the eight-hour day or the minimum wage, was incapable of being decided by discussion, the state had stepped in to impose a settlement by legislation.

If there was no big labor problem to be faced in 1931, there was also no need hurriedly to improvise schemes for large-scale relief. From the sixteenth century onward the care of the poor and needy has been recognized as a public obligation, to be met out of funds raised by taxation. Friendly societies and trade unions, as they grew up in the nineteenth century, spent the whole or a large part of their time and money caring for their sick, aged, or unemployed members. Membership in them was a voluntary act of insurance, and the extension of this voluntary insurance into national compulsory schemes was one of the greatest steps in the social politics of the modern world.

Germany pioneered in the field of insurance against sickness, accident, invalidity, and old age, but left Britain to experiment in insurance against the loss of income in time of unemployment. That experiment began in a small way in 1911 with a few occupations and two million workers, but during and after the war its scope was extended to include all workers except those in agriculture, domestic work, the civil service, and the higher grades of clerical work. In 1930 some twelve million workers were insured, and three-fourths of the total employed population was thus protected against complete loss of income when out of work, just as it was against the loss from sickness by a health insurance scheme.

The original scheme was a cautious insurance contract. Employer, employee, and state contributed to a fund, from which benefits were paid at a flat rate for a limited

number of weeks. After the scope was extended the contractual character was diluted. The law was amended
fourteen times between 1920 and 1927, and with each
alteration unemployment insurance approached nearer
to a relief scheme financed by employers, wage-earners
who were at work, and the state. The period of benefit
was extended almost indefinitely, the amount was increased, and additional payments were made to those with
dependents. The drain on the fund was therefore great,
and had to be met by increasing contributions and borrowing from the Treasury. The scheme was £25,000,000
in debt by 1928, and £120,000,000 in 1931.

In spite of the defects and departures, no political
party or economic class wants the system abolished. It
has been worth its cost, and has probably been cheaper
and more efficiently managed than any relief scheme. It
has maintained a certain level of income and purchasing
power among the unemployed. The abuses at the fringe
must not blind us to the contractual character of the
greater part of the scheme, and some of the abuses have
recently been eliminated. In a small measure the payment
deserves the name of "dole"; but experience in Canada
and the United States suggests that the alternative is either
costly public works which make little impression on the
body of unemployment or direct relief which becomes
entirely a dole. If in the future some form of unemployment insurance is established in North America, the British experience will help by showing what benefits accrue
and what pitfalls must be avoided.

In the task of aiding and reforming the business and
credit structure Washington has found some of its knot-

tiest problems. Most of these Britain has escaped. She did not need to run to the aid of the banks, for they had their worst troubles a century ago, when the banking system consisted of the Bank of England and a great swarm of private banks owned by families and partnerships. These banks could issue their own notes, and as they did so to excess many of them crashed after Waterloo, and a further heavy mortality accompanied the great panic of 1825.

These disasters suggested that the small private bank was rarely adequate for the needs of rapidly growing large-scale industry and commerce, and that the right of note issue must be regulated. Stronger banks were obtained by permitting joint-stock banks to be established; the note issue was made a Bank of England monopoly and given a gold backing. The joint-stock banks grew rapidly, swallowed up the small banks, and established branches. Amalgamation then reduced the number of banks until 85 per cent of British deposits were in the hands of five big banks in 1919. These five had their branches scattered over the whole country; they were competently and cautiously managed, they worked together to some extent, while the Bank of England served as bankers' bank for them and, if necessary, as a brake.

Critics scolded them for lack of enterprise, for keeping chiefly to short-term commercial loans, and for reluctance in adopting ambitious plans to finance industry and the farmer, as was done in Germany and the United States. There is some ground for these criticisms, but in defense the banks can at least mention two solid facts: there has been no serious banking panic since 1867, and scarcely any large bank failure during the last forty years. Hence the government has not needed to hurry with props to hold up the banks or with axes to lop off the heads of their officials.

In a third important field — that of building up a staff for framing and administering policies — Britain did not need to act hurriedly. She had steadily been building up a brain trust over a period of at least eighty years; in fact, some Britons would say that she has three brain trusts. The first is in her legislature. A political career has long been one of the most attractive and even honored occupations, and while at least half of the members of every House of Commons during the last century have been insignificant men, there has always been a large nucleus fitted by ability, training, and inclination for a political career. Since cabinet ministers are chosen from the legislature, men who show talent may climb up into office, and since defeat of a party at the polls may not consign ministers to private life, but only to the opposition benches, the House of Commons has on both sides men with long parliamentary and administrative experience.

The second brain trust is imbedded in the civil service. Eighty years ago the country grew dissatisfied with a service riddled by incompetence and recruited by nepotism, favoritism, and the spoils system. Revelation of the results of this system led to drastic reform, with a Civil Service Commission to lift the filling of vacancies out of politics, and with competitive examinations. For the higher reaches of the service the examination is such as can be faced only by the best university graduates. Its level is perhaps about that of a stiff Ph. D. "written," and a candidate must be high up the list in order to get appointed to a post.

This plan has achieved good results. The salary, conditions of tenure, and opportunities for congenial work have been sufficiently attractive to give the government its choice among the best-trained minds of the country, and while the civil service has not been always quite as good as it says it is, it has proved, in the words of the late Lord Haldane, to be "the one civil service in the world that was capable of combining efficiency with liberalism." From its ranks one could staff half a dozen universities with first-class faculties. Some of its men stand high in any company; others have left the service after making their mark there, and shown their mettle in the fields of business, education, or elsewhere.[2] Cabinet ministers come and go, governments rise and fall, but this corps of men carries on, serving a Socialist, Liberal, or Conservative chief with equal fidelity and skill.

The third brain trust is the royal commission, a body set up by the government to study facts, collect evidence and opinions, and make recommendations on some specific issue submitted to it. It differs from the select committee, or from congressional committees, in that it is not composed solely of legislators. On its membership roll are men from both houses and all parties, but publi-

[2] Mr. R. G. Hawtrey of the Treasury ranks among the leading currency and credit authorities of the world. Mr. Keynes's first job was in the India Office; Sir Josiah Stamp was an inland revenue officer before he stepped out to manage the Nobel Explosives Trust, run the biggest British railroad, and sit on the board of the Bank of England. Sir William Beveridge helped to establish the labor exchanges and unemployment insurance and to manage wartime food control before becoming head of the London School of Economics.

cists, scholars, business men, captains of industry, and labor leaders are also included. Witnesses and representatives of different economic groups or schools of thought give evidence, and the commission eventually reaches a body — or bodies — of recommendations which it submits to the government. Sometimes its proposals are unpalatable to the party in power, and the report is shelved; but many reports become important state papers, upon which new policies have been based or old ones amended.

It will now be clear that any British government facing the crisis had a much simpler task than did President Roosevelt. Many other factors combined to ease the task further. A country with an unwritten constitution did not have to worry much about the constitutionality of the decrees of its legislature. Whatever parliament decided should be law became law, and no court could tell the lawmakers they had exceeded their powers. With freedom of action went power of speedy action, for a cabinet that had a good majority could claim nearly all parliament's time for the measures it submitted, could limit discussion, and get a vote after brief debate.

A small country with one legislature did not face the complexities that confront North America through the existence of state and federal laws, separate state and national banking systems, etc. It had plenty of sectional interests and conflicts to disturb attempts at national unity, but they were not quite so divergent as those that characterize our debtor and creditor areas, our South, East, and Middle West. There were no groups quite comparable in their influence to the veterans, the silver bloc, or the embattled farmers, though some are gathering strength now that the country has embarked on a policy of tariffs, quotas, and subsidies.

More important still, there was little lingering faith in any doctrine of economic individualism or in the sanctity of inalienable natural rights where economic matters are concerned. The theory of natural rights went overboard early in the nineteenth century; in fact, it never got its feet so firmly planted on the political deck in England as in France and the United States. Experience with the new economic order of industrial capitalism soon showed that the rights of all individuals were not best fostered by a policy of laissez faire. As society grew more complicated and interdependent, the need for control at vital points made state action inevitable. Hence both the old political parties have long lists of social legislation to their credit, and while the Labor party accuses them of being "tools of the capitalist class" its practical program, as distinct from its ultimate objectives, differs only in degree from those of its opponents. In the eyes of all, rugged individualism is an ideal unsuited to a world in which men live and work close together.

From the above analysis one might draw the conclusion that a British cabinet had little to do when depression came, and could enjoy long week-end holidays while Washington was working overtime. The chapters which follow will correct any such conclusion. Britain did not have to face some of the problems that confronted America, but she had to face others; and some of her attempted solutions have involved breaches with the past quite as wide as have the recent policies of Washington.

CHAPTER TWO

BRITAIN'S PROBLEM

IN THE PREVIOUS CHAPTER WE SAW THAT RECOVERY IN-
volves the regaining of something that has been lost in
the depression, or the gaining of some compensating occupation for capital and labor to take its place. Viewed
in this light, Britain's problem is that of regaining the
ground lost, especially in her export markets, since 1929,
and of replacing some of that loss by expanding production for the home market. Since 1929 world trade has
fallen about 30 per cent in volume and nearly 70 per cent
in value. This collapse inflicted terrible damage on all
countries that depend largely on external markets, and
of that damage Britain received a full share. But even before 1929 she was wrestling with the same problem and
trying to win back markets lost by her big export industries during and after the war. Her problem was not created in 1929; it was only intensified, as the efforts made
to solve it during the preceding decade were more than
nullified.

Let us examine it a little more closely. For more than
three centuries Britain's economic history has been in
large and growing measure that of an exporter of minerals and manufactured goods. She began with woolen
cloth, lead, tin, hardware, and coal. She led in mechanical
invention and the harnessing of steam power, and for a
large part of the nineteenth century was the workshop

of the world. She put her steamships on the ocean lanes and sent her coal overseas to feed them. She invested her capital in the development of the new world north and south of the Equator, in colonies and foreign lands alike. London succeeded Amsterdam as the world's financier, banking, insuring, accepting, and discounting for men in every continent. All this gave employment to her people, and brought her in return the raw materials she could not produce and the foodstuffs she needed for her crowded urban population.

Great Britain was thus "the most international of all countries, most completely merged . . . in the world's economy, most dependent upon overseas trade."[1] How much of her work was done for overseas buyers we cannot say exactly. An estimate for 1924 said that 27 per cent of the value of all goods produced went abroad, and that the wages and salaries paid for making these exports were about one-eighth of the total wages and salary bill of the country. These figures, like similar estimates for the United States, conceal a great variety of conditions. The American dairy farmer does not worry about the foreign consumer, since we export no butter; but the cotton- and tobacco-growers do. Similarly, many British industries were essentially domestic in character, but others were deeply involved in the health and buying power of overseas customers.

Of the latter, textiles, iron and steel, machinery, and coal headed the list. In 1913 one-third of the coal output went overseas in ships' bunkers or as an export com-

[1] W. H. Beveridge, in *The World's Economic Crisis and the Way of Escape* (1932), p. 166.

modity. The cotton industry made nearly nine billion linear yards of fabric and exported seven billion of them. Seven billion yards is nearly four million miles, two-thirds of which went to clothe the Far East, especially India and China. The old woolen industry was more restrained in its efforts, yet it shipped overseas a hundred thousand miles of cloth. The iron and steel makers sent more than a quarter of their product abroad, the engineers had a large external market, the shipyards built two-thirds of the world's new ships, and the shipowners possessed two-fifths of the world's tonnage.

To the Englishman this exchange of his manufactures and financial or shipping services for food and raw materials from other countries accorded with that territorial specialization which the textbooks blessed as the highest and wisest economy. He had shown his faith in that economy by leaving agriculture to sink or swim in the currents of cheap wool, butter, bacon, and grain that flowed in from outside and by exposing his own manufactures and ships to whatever competition might come from any quarter. But some of his customers did not share his belief, and for four decades before the war his place in the world economy, and the economy itself, were being challenged. The industrial rise of the United States, Germany, and Japan gave the world four workshops, and showed that there was nothing to prevent countries which had the necessary resources from building their own industries. Outside the "big four," smaller or newer political units were bending their energies toward manufacturing development and seeking protection behind tariff walls.

The war and the years that followed accentuated the desire for economic self-sufficiency to a degree probably never before known in the world's history. Hostilities cut the contacts between buyers and sellers, either because the buyers were now enemies or because the sellers were too busy making war supplies and had no goods to spare for export or ships in which to carry them. The buyers turned to other sources of supply such as Japan or the United States, or developed their own factories. When the war ended some of Britain's old markets were feeding themselves or were buying from non-European producers; they had an expanded and more diversified manufacturing equipment or were determined to have one as soon as possible; or their pockets were empty.

To lose markets is much easier than to win them back, and British export industries spent the twenties trying to regain their lost ground. Their success varied. Lancashire met powerful rivalry from Indian and Japanese mills in the eastern market. The Japanese had new efficient equipment, cheap labor, well-trained technicians, and a highly concentrated and integrated organization. Against their nine great producing units and three trading firms Lancashire pitted three thousand firms, no united front, much obsolete machinery, an overcapitalized structure, and high labor and other costs. The Indian mills were protected by a new tariff and by Mr. Gandhi's nationalist campaign, while the Chinese tariff was high enough to foster production there. Hence Lancashire's exports fell nearly half in yardage. The county still held about half the total world trade, especially that in fine qualities; but much of the great Oriental mass market for the cheap fabrics could not be won back. After 1929 the long twi-light deepened into night, and there is as yet little sign of dawn. The exports of 1933 were half those of the gloomy twenties, and in 1931 two cotton workers out of five were idle.

The woolen industry was hit hard and found recovery difficult. Foreign competition was keener, tariffs were higher. The short-dress era in women's fashions, the popularity of knitted wear, and the improvement of rayon reduced the demand. Between 1913 and 1931 ex-ports fell by half, and in the latter year three workers out of every ten were unemployed.

Coal was a sick industry in most countries. Oil fuel, the Diesel engine, the greater use of electricity, and the harnessing of falling water to produce hydro-electricity, all broke its monopoly, and those who still bought coal used it more economically. King Coal ceased to be a merry old soul, as his despotism was turned into a limited monarchy and as he lost many of his subjects. Domestic sales were reduced by depression in the heavy industries, and in foreign markets competition with Polish and Ger-man coal for the shrunken markets was intense. Yet the British output had crept back by 1929 to nine-tenths of its pre-war volume, and four-fifths of the export and bunker markets had been won back. But in that year one-sixth of the miners were still idle and the depression plunged output and exports down again. In 1932 one-third the coal workers lacked jobs.

Finally, the war and its sequel wrought havoc on the British metal trades. Shipbuilding boomed during the war in order to thwart the submarine; by 1921 the world's merchant tonnage was swollen far beyond the needs of ocean commerce, and the industry was glutted with shipyards and workers. During the next decade British shipowners did not expand their fleets, but other countries built up larger merchant marines and added to the excessive shipping supply. Unemployment was therefore high around British shipyards, even before 1929 virtually ended the ordering of vessels. The new tonnage launched in 1932 was one-tenth that of 1913, and two out of every three workers were idle.

A similar story can be told of iron, steel, and the engineering trades. Swollen in equipment and labor force by war, deflated by peace, facing keen competition and higher tariffs, these industries strove to win back markets. By 1929 the iron and steel makers had climbed back to nearly 90 per cent of their pre-war export level, but in 1932 they were below the 40 per cent mark, and nearly half their workers unemployed. The machine exporters had regained four-fifths of the lost ground by 1929, only to lose half their gains by 1932, when over half their employees were out of work.

The twenties thus saw Britain weakened where she had been strongest. About two-fifths of the standing army of a million unemployed belonged to these old industries, but their lack of work reacted on the fortunes of industries which had no direct contact with the outside world. Her depressed industries were depressed in many other countries, e. g., coal, shipbuilding, and some textiles in the United States; but her greater dependence on them made her feel the effects more severely than did other lands. In no single old export industry had the pre-war position been won back in 1929; the exuberant expansion of the nineteenth century was evidently ended, and the future offered at best stability, at worst senility.

In one field, that of capital investment abroad, Britain was by 1929 back to her pre-war position. For nearly a century she had been exporting loans and investments to provide new equipment for old countries or to finance the development of new ones. By 1914, £4,000,000,000 had been scattered over the face of the globe, a sum that was probably nearly a quarter of Britain's national wealth. During the war a quarter of these investments had to be sold to pay for munitions, but when peace came the export of capital was resumed, and by 1929 the amount invested overseas was as large as in 1913.

This vast export of capital had two main effects. In the first place much of it went out in the form of British manufactured goods and thus provided work for industries and ships, just as the export of American capital during the nineteen-twenties stimulated American industries and exports. In the second place, the interest or dividends, which in 1913 and 1929 amounted to about £250,000,000, might be left overseas for further investment or be transferred to Britain in the form of food and raw materials. Australia paid her interest in wool, metal, and wheat, Canada in wheat and metals, the Argentine in beef, New Zealand in butter and frozen lamb.

These payments explain in part a phenomenon which has puzzled casual observers for the last three hundred years and promises to do so for centuries to come. That phenomenon is the difference between the value of the goods a country exports and the value of those it imports. A country that buys more than it sells is either shrewd in persuading foreigners to give more than they get or, since all foreigners are subtle schemers, it is falling into a trap and will soon be skinned of its gold. An excess of exports is a favorable balance of trade and is good, an excess of imports is unfavorable and bad, calling for action to correct the balance or even tip it the other way.

Ever since 1854 Britain's balance has been unfavorable. The explanation is not that outsiders were simple or subtle, but that they were paying in goods what they owed, as well as for the goods and services they bought. For the goods she bought Britain could pay with the proceeds of those she sold, but those were not enough. To supplement them she had the money outsiders paid her for carrying their goods or persons on British ships, insurance premiums on policies written by British companies, commissions to financial or commercial agents, interest and sinking fund on overseas loans, and dividends on investments. The loans and investments gave her an external buying power of about £250,000,000, and the earnings from shipping, banking, and insurance nearly as much. Hence she could buy far more than she sold, and still have credit left for further investment.

In 1929, according to a Board of Trade estimate, the visible exports of goods failed to pay for the visible imports of goods by about £380,000,000. But when the "invisible exports" had been placed against this figure, all the goods were paid for, and there was still £103,000,000 left over. This was a healthy position, but if the visible or invisible exports fell off or the visible imports increased too much it might become unhealthy. If the sale of British goods declined, if shipping and other earnings were reduced, if debtors defaulted or stocks failed to earn dividends, the plus sign might be turned into a minus, and the country would be unable to pay for its imports out of its current income.

This actually happened in 1931. The excess of imports rose a little, but the shipping income dropped by more than a third; defaults on interest and reductions or omissions of dividends cut the yield from these sources by nearly a third, and the other earnings declined nearly a half. The balance was therefore an adverse one of £104,000,000. This situation might be met by borrowing, by selling securities, or by exporting gold. The last method was impossible, for it would have swallowed up over half the country's total gold reserve in one year; the two other methods meant living on one's capital. Realization of the state to which the country's external trade and business activity had sunk was in part responsible for the abandonment of free trade. If exports were too small, imports must be checked: if the country could not sell, ship, and collect, it must buy less.

Enough has been said to explain the character of the British depression. The export industries were sick before 1929, but some of them were slowly regaining strength when the collapse of world trade plunged them into a severe relapse. In some respects their story resembles that of American agriculture during the postwar years. But their story is not the whole tale. While the American farmer was struggling to get out of the Slough of Despond some American industries were rushing ahead; while the old brigade of British industry was nursing its wounds other industries, especially those which served the domestic market, were faring much better before 1929, and have recovered most since 1932.

Some of these industries produce goods or render services that have become prominent in the western world since the war. The automobile, a good road on which to run it, the radio, the cinema, the whole range of electrical appliances, phonographs, bicycles, rayon, confectionery, and cosmetics, all are conveniences, comforts, or luxuries that post-war England wished to enjoy nearly as much as North America did. It had not as much money to spare for them, but it had enough to create a substantial demand, and enough contact with North American consumption habits to stimulate that demand still further. Its birth rate had fallen a third since pre-war days, and as parents had fewer children to feed, dress, and rear, some of the income that once would have bought necessaries was now available for comforts and luxuries. Further, there had been a marked redistribution of income. The rich and the middle class were poorer than in pre-war days, largely because of heavy taxation, but the poor — especially those in the lower wage classes — were much less poor. Some of the higher wages of the war period had remained, and the wage level generally did not fall as prices fell during the twenties.

Except for the homes of those who carried the burden of unemployment and of the depressed industries, the standard of living, dress, food, leisure, and pleasure was materially much higher in 1928 or 1931 than in 1914. Mill girls had discarded clogs, cotton stockings, and shawls, and donned shoes, rayon hose, coats, and hats.

Few homes lacked a phonograph or radio, few boys lacked bicycles, every other young man seemed to have a motorcycle, while the better-paid artisans and the middle class were beginning to own cars. The cinema was almost as popular as across the Atlantic, canned fruits and vegetables were releasing winter meals from the tyranny of prunes, dried peas, and Brussels sprouts, while pastrycook, candy, and tobacco stores had lavish displays unknown in 1914. Holidays were being taken further afield, leisure time was being spent away from home or the tavern, and thrift was being directed toward the purchase of homes by young people whose parents could never have become more than tenants.

This trend in consumption habits was reflected in the employment statistics, for while the number of insured workers in the stagnant or shrinking occupations dropped more than half a million between 1923 and 1930, that in the expanding trades — especially distribution, building, road transport, motor manufacture and service, printing, rayon, and the electrical industries — rose by 1,750,000. The trend was also seen in the shift of industry and population from the north and west, the home of Victorian industrialism, to the south and east, and especially to the hinterland of London. The new industries do not need great quantities of coal, but use electric power; the raw material is usually not heavy and can be brought by sea, rail, or road to London. The metropolis is the largest single market for the product as well as the hub of the transport system. The climate is better than in the north, the trade unions are not so strong. Hence the post-war industrial development of the south has been as marked as the stagnation of the north. Even the university towns have been stirred; Cambridge makes one of the best-known radios, and Oxford is a suburb of a large automobile-building center.

If it had been possible to transfer workers from the coal fields, shipyards, and cotton towns to these new industries, or if the pre-war stream of emigration had begun to flow in its old volume when peace came, the pains of post-war readjustment might have been greatly allayed. But the day of mass emigration from Europe seems to have ended; the greater cost of the sea passage, the imposition of immigration restrictions, and the disappearance of the frontier have reduced emigration to insignificant dimensions. Internal migration was not easy, for men who had grown to middle age in the coal and cotton towns were as loath to leave these devastated areas as are some of the farmers of the drought-stricken Dakotas.

If the new industries could have won a place in the export markets, Britain's position in world trade might have been strengthened. But in these industries she had no advantage over her chief competitors, and in some of them was at a disadvantage because she started late or because her home market was too small to permit mass production. Rayon could be made as easily in France, Germany, or the United States. The latter country was ahead of Britain in the production of electrical equipment and automobiles, and its exports were able to take advantage of the economies of mass production for a great home market. Hence the new products of the post-war decade could do little to take the place of the old ones in filling the holds of outgoing steamers.

CHAPTER THREE

EARLY SEARCHES FOR SOLUTIONS

IF BRITAIN'S RECOVERY PROBLEM GOES BACK TO THE END of the war, her search for solutions began long before 1931, and some of her efforts since that year have carried on policies formulated in the twenties. Britain had its depressed industries, as America had its farm problem, and in each country the air was thick with plans.

These were of two kinds. The first sought salvation through the removal of external obstacles by international cooperation. Trade would revive of its own accord if only the economic folly of the reparations claims could be cast aside, if currency muddles were straightened out, if interallied debts were liquidated, and if the rush toward economic nationalism were checked. When war passions cooled, when Germany and Austria were restored as producers and purchasers, then customers would return to the old store. At an international conference at Geneva in 1927 British delegates pleaded for an end to the widespread raising of tariffs, and in 1929 suggested a conference to discuss a general tariff truce; but that conference met too late — in March, 1930. In fact there was nearly always some conference just ahead, after which the sun would shine.

The second kind of policy found the causes of depression nearer home, in the defective structure and methods of British industry. The word "rationalization" was popular in psychology and economics, and when men asked "What's wrong with British industry?" the answer often was that it was irrationally organized. Its structure might have been adequate to the demands of the comfortable nineteenth century but was unsuited to the needs of the twentieth. There were too many small units, competing fiercely with each other and with their larger rivals abroad. There were too many middlemen handling goods as they passed along the chain of production and sale. There was too much antiquated and obsolete equipment, and too many mines or factories were operating at half capacity in place of a few giant units working at full pressure. There was too much conservatism, worship of traditional methods, individualism, third-generation indolence and incompetence.

If capital was stupid, labor was stubborn. Wage rates were kept rigid and inflexible by strong collective bargaining methods, and reductions were difficult in time of depression or of falling prices. The increase of real wages since the war had accentuated the British worker's position as the best-paid employee in Europe, but it was not accompanied by a proportionate increase in productivity. In the sheltered industries wage rates remained high, and the cost of the service they rendered to exporters was therefore a heavy burden on the backs of men who had to fight German or Polish rivals. The high rate of interest that follows every long war and the heavy local and national taxes reduced the supply of capital available for reinvestment and expansion, and after 1925 the restoration of the gold standard with the pound at its old value was harmful to exporters. Finally, some industries had too much water in their capital stock: they could never be worked profitably until some of the water was squeezed out.

Much of this diagnosis was correct, especially when applied to the older industries. Happy was the industry that had no history. There was need for medical and surgical treatment, for remodeling and rejuvenation. But we may doubt whether a management composed of dictatorial efficiency experts and a labor force willing to cooperate and submit in every way could have done much better in regaining the old prosperity in face of exchange difficulties, growing economic nationalism, oil fuel, new fashions, new commodities, the expansion of the United States, and the poverty of some customers.

If treatment was needed, industry could try to cure itself and the state might play some part. Mr. Fay has called the period 1922–1932 a "decade of rationalization," and the label fits the earlier years as well as the later. In 1921 the government gave the country its first big dose of economic reorganization when it released the railroads from wartime control. That control had brought unified management to twenty-six chief and ninety-three subsidiary railroad companies; the economies had been great, and Labor urged that the railroads remain unified and become a state enterprise; but the stockholders wanted their property back. They had their way, but the roads came back to them in four large units, not in a hundred and nineteen. Had the stockholders foreseen the damage which the motor vehicle and depression were to inflict on railroad profits, they might have been more socialistic than was Labor.

The coal industry, Britain's second largest industry — agriculture comes first — was subjected to almost unbroken attention by the state. The importance of coal exports to British trade and the strength of the miners' unions made the welfare of the industry a national concern. Two royal commissions in six years examined the patient, and pointed out the anarchy in production and sale caused by the operation of over three thousand mines by fifteen hundred firms. To bring order, effect economies, and restore prosperity, drastic reorganization was necessary. Firms must amalgamate in larger units, small or inefficient mines must be closed, cutthroat competition must be prevented, and marketing must be controlled by agreement among producers or by the establishment of selling agencies.

There was some voluntary response to these recommendations, but not much. When depression came, parliament therefore stepped in, and in 1930 the Coal Mines Act was passed to establish machinery for the regulation of production and sale, to fix quotas, to promote the preparation of reorganization schemes, and generally put the industry on a sounder basis. The fact that reorganization meant combination, trusts, or cartels, and that free enterprise was to be limited, no longer scared the planners. Competition in a glutted market was deadly; the unpleasant effects of combination could be no worse than the unpleasant aspects of the new competition, and perhaps they might be prevented by skillful control.

The task of remodeling was entrusted to a Reorganization Commission, whose business was to induce mine owners to prepare schemes; but if they failed to do this the Commission had power to prepare its own plans. In its report issued late in 1933, the Commission described the job still ahead of it as follows: "The crying need of the industry is for planned coordination of all its phases — development, production, treatment, marketing and research." The need was "crying" because "the picture now presented by the greater part of the industry is one of haphazard development of each coal field by a large number of uncoordinated units brought into existence on no rational plan, nearly all working below capacity, competing suicidally, whether in capital expenditure or in prices, or both, for a market that cannot absorb the product of all." It would be cheaper to make a levy on the better pits and use the money to close the poor ones. Then the active mines could set up a central authority to coordinate their selling policy and look after development and research.

In some areas mine owners have prepared schemes, and the Commission has power to impose plans accepted by a majority of producers on the recalcitrant owners. In other areas the Commission is still engaged in "fanning an uncertain spark of voluntary effort"; in others no spark has yet been struck and the Commission is therefore preparing its own plans. Quite evidently a decade of discussion and three years of official action have achieved little.

In one other place, not this time a sickbed, the state made an attempt at rationalization. The public supply of electricity was in the hands of municipal authorities and private companies, while some factories made their own power. Defective laws prevented neighboring towns from building joint power stations; production was usually on a small scale, prices were high, electric light was rarely seen outside the homes of urban well-to-do people, and industrial consumption was small. In 1919 an attempt was made to coordinate the public and private producers. But the two were like oil and water; they would not mix. In 1926 therefore a Conservative government took one of those steps toward a combination of public and private enterprise that had marked the development of public utilities in other parts of Europe.

A Central Electricity Board was set up to undertake the public construction of a national system of high-tension distribution lines, covering the whole country with a grid. Electrical generation was to be concentrated in a number of great power stations, and hundreds of small inefficient plants were to be closed. No profit was to be made on generation or transmission, for the power was to be sold at cost to the existing public and private retailers. The whole scheme was to be finished by 1940, but by early 1934 nearly half the area and three-fourths of the population had been "gridded," and electrical consumption had doubled in eight years.

At other points government action tried to help industry. In 1928 the load of local taxation was reduced. Local taxes were levied chiefly on property rather than on income, and it was felt that the burden they imposed on some industries, including agriculture, was killing the bearers. Some of the cost of local government was therefore transferred to the shoulders of the central government, to be met out of revenue drawn from income tax, customs, excise, and other national taxes. The problem that Britain tried in this way to solve is well known in the United States and Canada; local tax systems inherited from the days when most property was real estate and most activity agricultural do not fit the needs of industrial and commercial societies.

Apart from these efforts, the sick industries had to be left to cure themselves. The road to convalescence was long and steep, and government action could do little to shorten the journey, especially when the way to external markets lay beyond the territorial bounds of its sovereignty. If those who served these markets persisted in retaining their individuality the state must either leave them to work out their own salvation or impose a heavy hand on them, and this it was loath to do. The doctrine of a later day, that governments should force minorities to conform to plans supported by majorities, had not yet won sufficient favor, and few industries had a majority that had reached agreement on any plan. Even if they had, reorganization and re-equipment called for new capital, and a sick industry was unattractive to investors or lenders. The Bank of England did sponsor the establishment of a Bankers' Industrial Development Company, which was to provide the necessary capital for cotton, shipbuilding, and other ailing industries, but the results were small and unspectacular.

If little could be done to salvage capital, less could be done for labor. In 1928 the country at large awoke to the fact that depression, reinforced by a certain measure of rationalization and the closing of "redundant" plants, had dotted parts of Wales, Lancashire, Durham, and Scotland with dead and derelict areas. Pits had been abandoned and would never again be worked; shipyards were rusting. No new industries were coming in to take the place of the old, and the folk who had been trapped in these places were scraping together a bare existence. They could not emigrate, for the new world did not want their kind of labor; they could not afford to migrate if the family was large; and they were not sure that their kind of skill or their strange speech would be welcome in the south.

Description of these grim conditions led to an intensification of efforts that had already been made to train cast-off workers for new jobs and to transfer them to regions where industry was expanding. An Industrial Transference Board, a Mansion House Relief Fund, and the Quakers played a part. Training depots were opened for men under thirty-five years of age and "reconditioning centers" were set up. But the coming of the general depression and the exhaustion of funds checked this work almost as soon as it had begun; by March, 1934, only 120,000 persons had been moved from these "areas without a future." Water ran into the mine faster than it was pumped out, and the problem became more difficult and urgent than ever.

Its tragic aspects have been described by two recent observers. Mr. J. B. Priestley in his *English Journey* tells of these industrially devastated areas as he saw them in 1933. In Blackburn he found the ruins of an industry that once made cheap cottons for the loincloths of India's hundreds of millions, saw mills that had cost £100,000 fail to draw a single bid in the auction room, heard of cotton kings who were now picking up cigarette ends in the streets, and talked to weavers who had not touched a loom for four years. The factory chimneys had not smoked for so long that the bricks and stones were beginning to be washed clean and the air was becoming fresh.[1]

In similar vein a special correspondent of the *Times* wrote of what he saw in Durham in March, 1934. In the whole county 37 men out of every 100 were workless; around a spot with the picturesque name of Bishop Auckland 58 were idle while 42 worked. In Jarrow, once a prosperous shipyard town of 32,000 souls, 75 were out of work for every 25 who were in. In some places every pit had been abandoned, and "the price obtainable for coking coal is never likely to justify the cost of renovating them and working the reserves which remain." The wealth obtained from them in the past has made no provision for evil days, and "those who will have to answer for Durham on the day of judgment are the directors of the colliery companies."[2] Whether modern society can afford to wait till then may be doubted; meanwhile the derelict miners and cotton weavers, like the submarginal farmers of America, present a problem of salvage which may tax to the full the efforts of the state and private enterprise.

While the war gave Britain some sick industries it also gave her some infant industries, and in nurturing these the country made its first departure from the policy of free trade adopted in the second quarter of the nineteenth century. In 1915 duties of 33⅓ per cent were

[1] J. B. Priestley, *English Journey* (1934), pp. 213 ff. and Chapter 10.
[2] *Times Weekly Edition*, March 22, 1934.

placed on imported motor vehicles and some other commodities, partly to check the influx of luxuries and partly to conserve shipping space. In 1921 duties were levied to "safeguard" certain "key industries" which had grown up and were supplying essential articles formerly imported from Germany. Anti-dumping duties were placed on some goods that were being offered at low prices because of depreciated currency. In 1922 protection was given the beet sugar industry, and later a subsidy was added. In 1919 the policy of imperial preference was adopted; dutiable imports were admitted free or at two-thirds the general rate if they came from the overseas empire.

During the next ten years tariff policy fluctuated. The Conservatives wished to go further, the Labor and Liberal parties wanted to retreat, and when the opinion of the electorate was sought the verdict favored the traditional policy of free imports. But the early steps were never fully retraced when free traders sat on the government benches, and in 1930 the customs list contained duties that were purely for revenue purposes, purely protective levies, compromises between the two, and preferential treatment of Empire produce.

Those who fought the battle of imperial preference stressed the services of the dominions and colonies during the war, pleaded for shopping inside the family, and pointed to the preference already given Great Britain in the dominion tariffs. Some of them had visions of a self-sufficing empire, with Britain as the manufacturer and shipper and the dominions as primary producers. Like good Cobdenites they saw the advantages of this regional specialization and talked of free trade—within the Empire. They hoped that Britain could repair the damaged fabric of her foreign trade by expanding her sales to the children, and urged that she turn her back on the rest of the world, much as the advocates of "America self-contained" do in the United States.

Unfortunately for such dreams, Canada and Australia were among the world's most aggressive economic nationalists, determined to build up their manufactures and to grant only such preference as would still leave a highly protective wall against the goods Britain most desired to sell them. Further, the only substantial preference Britain could grant them would be on foods and raw materials, and she could do this only by taxing the two-thirds of her imported supply that she drew from outside the Empire for the benefit of the one-third she bought within. Finally, abandonment of the foreign market was a gospel of despair. In 1913 and in 1923 about one-third of Britain's exports went to imperial markets; the rest of the world bought two-thirds of them, and no expansion within the Empire could conceivably compensate for the loss of that market.

These considerations acted as a brake on the efforts of Empire enthusiasts. But perhaps family buying could be stimulated without taxes on foreign foods, and in 1925 the Empire Marketing Board was established to stimulate, by publicity and research, the demand in Britain for home-grown and Empire-grown produce. For eight years the Board gently and artistically sought to interest the consumer in the national origin of the goods he bought. Its displays on a thousand billboards were fine examples of commercial art; its films depicting various Empire industries, its research and its information services, were of a high order. As an experiment in the education of the consumer it probably did one of the best pieces of publicity ever accomplished — and all with funds which in America we should call a shoestring. But the task of making purchase an act of patriotism was one for Hercules.

Against the many efforts to meet and solve post-war problems must be placed one that probably undid much of the good done by other attempts. In 1925 Great Britain returned to the gold standard with the pound at its pre-war parity. Some experts had urged that the value of the pound be not fixed, and pleaded the case for a managed currency. Others said, "Fix it at a lower level than its pre-war value, say at $4.00, or $4.20, instead of at $4.86." But the final decision favored the old figure, and on May 1, 1925, the pound could once more "look the dollar in the face."

If some took pride in, and gained profit from, that decision, others paid for it. Those who were creditors and had lent pounds abroad now received $4.86 in place of the $3.50 (or thereabouts) which had come to them when the pound was down. But exporters found that their goods became dearer to foreign buyers as the pound recovered, since those buyers had to give more francs, dollars, or marks to secure a pound's worth of goods. British goods became more costly in the foreign market and were therefore less able to compete with those from other places. The British price level was too high in pounds of the 1925 value and must be lowered if goods were to be sold abroad, while foreign goods were now cheaper than they had been and could therefore enter the British market more easily. Mr. Fay says that coal exporters received 10 per cent less in sterling than they had done a short time before, and they knew, better than any other kind of employer, how difficult it was to reduce wages in face of falling prices.

The advocates of a managed currency argued that the restoration of the gold standard would sacrifice productive industry and export trade to metropolitan finance, and there is a good case for declaring that the credit controllers of the country sought to maintain, or win back, the financial supremacy of London at the expense of British industry. For this they were not entirely blameworthy, as they could not foresee how the gold standard was going to behave or how London had lost the power to control that behavior.

In pre-war days all financial roads led to London. A Belgian banker has well described the "enormous and active reservoir of capital" that London had become. "Admirably organized, strong in knowledge and in traditions proved twenty times over, able to keep its head in times of difficulty and to help others even by assuming for itself an excess of risk, organized to respond to the infinite diversity of the needs of international commerce — the market of the City was in truth the masterpiece of an incomparable and delicate mechanism for the distribution of products throughout the world." [3]

Of those products gold was only a very small part. It moved but little from country to country, and Great

[3] P. van Zeeland, *A View of Europe, 1932* (1933), p. 3.

Britain in 1913 could conduct its business with less than £40,000,000 gold reserve in the Bank of England and £120,000,000 in circulation or in the hands of the other banks. This total was about one-fifth of the gold held in the United States in 1929. If there was need for more gold, the Bank of England pressed a button — it raised the bank rate — and gold came in from outside to take advantage of this higher interest rate. If there was a plethora of gold the Bank pressed another button, lowered its rate, and the gold flowed out. The important fact was that in effect there was only one set of buttons.

After the war there were three sets, for London had to share control with Paris and New York. Dual control might be feasible, but triple control was almost impossible, especially when gold developed the mobility of a globule of mercury on a sheet of polished glass. It ran about restlessly as the glass was tipped now this way, now that. Had its movements represented long-term investments there might have been little cause for worry; but often they were short-term loans or were deposits made by some foreigner who was dodging a bank failure or currency inflation or taking advantage of a high call money rate in Wall Street. The general flow was toward Paris and New York, and those who had to operate a central bank in London with a gold supply liable to sudden deposits or withdrawals must expect anxious moments.

Those moments came in 1929 and 1931. The crisis of 1929 in England was precipitated partly by a heavy drain on the Bank's gold reserves in 1928–1929. The crisis of July and August, 1931, was largely due to an infectious series of raids on gold supplies. The Bank of England had lent money to German and Austrian banks. These were raided by their depositors and had to declare a moratorium. The British loans therefore could not be repaid, but meanwhile Frenchmen and Americans grew nervous over their deposits in London and began to withdraw them. In one week in July, 1931, the Bank of England lost nearly one-eighth of its gold.

The gold standard was thus endangered. The slender supply of liquid resources on which it rested was leaking rapidly. Efforts to check the flight from the pound failed, in spite of large grants of credit by Paris and New York. This crisis came just at the time when a gaping deficit in the public accounts became apparent, and when a committee reported that the country's income for 1931–1932 would fall short of its expenditure by the huge sum of £120,000,000. Thus with private and public finances in dire straits, Britain came to her crisis. Two years of depression had swept away the ground she had regained in her foreign trade and much more. Her domestic market, the only large world emporium into which goods could freely or easily pour, was being inundated by distress selling of foreign wares. Her unemployment figures were mounting from the second toward the third million. Her crushing taxes were proving inadequate to meet the cost of government, and her banking and financial system was being subjected to a tremendous strain. It was August, but happily not the fourth of August.

Much that has happened since has been influenced by the effect of the crisis on the personnel of government and on the temper of the public. The Labor cabinet learned that in order to obtain a foreign loan it must

reduce certain expenditures and make a 10 per cent reduction in the payments to the unemployed. This was
unpalatable to those cabinet members and legislators who
depended largely on trade union money and votes for
their election, and also to others who felt that the limits
of taxation had not been reached or that dictation from
bankers should be resisted. If the pound could be saved
only by cutting the wages of government employees and
the pittance to the unemployed, it was not worth saving.
The cabinet was split. Mr. MacDonald resigned, and then
formed a "National" government containing a majority
of Conservatives, some Labor men, and some Liberals.
A budget of drastic cuts and increased taxes was rushed
through, two foreign loans were obtained, but the drain
on gold continued, and one Monday morning in late
September, 1931, we opened our morning papers to learn
that England had gone off the gold standard. We read
that news with much the same feeling as on the morning
of March 4, 1933, we read the announcement that every
bank in the United States was closed.

The overthrow of the Labor cabinet paved the way
for an "axe and tax" budget, but failed to save the pound.
What next? The new government had ample parliamentary support for any steps it cared to take, but for
reasons which were probably adequate, without being at
all clear, it decided on an election. It asked in vague general terms for power to save the country from bankruptcy, and for a "doctor's mandate" to diagnose and
then prescribe. It got what it asked for, and rarely has
a nation delivered itself so completely into a doctor's
hands.

The vote that swept Labor aside largely reflected a belief that the Labor cabinet had quitted its post when the weather grew murky because it was afraid of the union leaders in the fo'castle. Labor gathered seven million votes, its opponents sixteen millions, but owing to electoral methods the seven millions won only fifty seats, while the sixteen millions won over five hundred and fifty. The middle classes, which had been growing increasingly sympathetic toward Labor, reversed their opinion, and many wage-earners did the same.

The result was thus one of those landslides that seem to characterize modern — or at least modern depression — elections. The American election of 1932, the election in British Columbia in 1933, and those in Nova Scotia, Saskatchewan, and Ontario in 1934 all showed similar results. The party which had held office was routed, and its opponent was given an overwhelming strength, thanks to which it could do what it wished with no effective opposition. This may be the English-speaking world's substitute for dictatorship. Under the parliamentary system the cabinet can go ahead, assured of prompt acceptance of its plans by the legislature; and under certain conditions the presidential system may see the same concentration of initiative in the executive branch of the government.

British policy was now in the hands of a government which had not to worry about a gold standard and which had virtually complete freedom to do what it wished until its time expired in 1936. Behind it in the House of Commons was a party composed largely of raw recruits, new to the game of politics, and overwhelmingly Conservative in complexion. There was a liberal sprinkling of economic jingoes, of business men who were determined to see that their region or industry got what it wanted, and of landlords who after a long walk in the dust were now back in their natural place — the saddle. Outside was a nation roused to consciousness of crisis, stirred to a sense of national danger as if war had come again, willing to "grin and bear," ready to drink whatever medicine the government said was best for it, but with a capacity for criticism and for crying "fiddlesticks" that was not for long dulled or restrained.

CHAPTER FOUR

THE BRITISH NEW DEAL

THE CROWDED YEARS SINCE AUGUST, 1931, DESTROY ANY belief that the British government has been letting nature take its course in lifting the country out of depression. We have seen that Britain need not do certain things, since they were done already, and that she could not do certain others. But there were still many tasks her rulers felt they must tackle, in the fields of currency and credit, of commercial policy, of national finance, of production and distribution, and of labor problems. There has been relief, reform, regulation, reorganization, protection, subsidies, and at some points an extension of state control that deserves the label of regimentation. The British schoolboy can lament that a lot of new history has been piled up for him to learn, and the advocate of liberty has cause for disquiet.

The tangled story can best be examined under four headings — national finance, currency and credit policy, trade policy, and miscellaneous aids and reforms. The present chapter examines the first two and part of the third, but one aspect of trade policy, caused by the rediscovery of the British farmer, calls for a chapter of its own.

1. National Finance. — No American reader needs to be told that in recent years his taxes have become much heavier, but perhaps he may be consoled with the knowledge that this is a universal phenomenon. For many years prior to 1934 a British budget speech was a sickbed talk, almost a funeral oration, with its tale of deficits or small surpluses, and its demand for a continuance of high taxes or for still higher ones. A pre-war Chancellor of the Exchequer could pay his way if he collected about £170,000,000, but Mr. Snowden needed £800,000,000 in 1931. The national debt had been multiplied twelve-fold by the war; the interest on it, the pensions to veterans, and the cost of defense amounted to £500,000,000, which was over 60 per cent of the public revenue and over £12 a year for every man, woman, and child in the country. In addition there were the costs of running what has been called "the social service state," of providing for education, public health, old-age pensions, insurance, and so forth, at a cost of £200,000,000.

A post-war central government must therefore collect between £700,000,000 and £800,000,000 each year. When to this was added the demands of local governments, the British people paid between a fifth and a quarter of their pre-depression income to the tax collector. When depression deepened and incomes fell, this fraction rose higher, and still the revenue was inadequate. In April, 1931, Mr. Snowden budgeted for a deficit of £38,000,000, but hoped that the overdue trade revival would soon come, bring him more revenue, and thus wipe out this deficit. He gambled on an early turn of the tide, and lost his bet. Conditions grew worse, and by August it was evident that the deficit would amount to £120,000,000 instead of £38,000,000.

In the light of our own recent deficits this sum may

seem small. To orthodox Britons, accustomed to paying for current expenses out of current revenue, it was a warning that the country was living beyond its means. The living must therefore be made less costly, and the means must be augmented. A revised budget was submitted, based on the slogan "Axe and tax." Income tax rates were raised still higher, exemptions and allowances for dependents were reduced, and small incomes were made subject to the tax. Cabinet ministers' salaries were reduced 10 to 20 per cent, as were those of judges and officers in the crown services. Members of parliament lost a tenth of their "allowance"; teachers, policemen, soldiers, sailors, and all ranks of the public service lost up to a tenth of their pay. Finally, the benefits paid to the unemployed were reduced one-tenth.

Such a program hurt far and wide. As one read it, thoughts about straws on camels' backs could not be brushed aside. The first installment of Britain's new deal looked like a raw deal. If this drastic budget failed to make ends meet, what then? If people could not meet their tax demands, what then? The first question only time could answer. The second was answered thus by an income tax official in February, 1932: a final demand for payment of income tax must be met within seven days, or distraint or summary proceedings would follow. The collector had full power to walk in and distrain on the goods and chattels of the defaulter. "If the defaulter bolts the door, the collector has a warrant to open the door forcibly and enter. . . . There is no softheartedness. The collector must get the money. If, when the goods are sold, there is any money left over, it is returned to the taxpayer."[1] The Englishman has been schooled into paying taxes when they are due, and tax default is a rare and fruitless sin.

The budget burdens of August, 1931, remained unchanged till 1934. How they hurt, only those who were in the country at the time can realize; but since they were inevitable, and since there was some rough attempt to achieve equality of sacrifice, people paid while they grumbled. After the strain and pain of the war, nothing could ever be unbearable again. Yet for two years the budget did not balance, and only in 1934 could the Chancellor of the Exchequer give some relief to his victims.

That relief came on the heels of a surplus of nearly £40,000,000.[2] In two and a half years the national accounts had improved by £200,000,000, and the Chancellor was consequently able to ease the strain on those who had suffered most in 1931. He cut the income tax by 10 per cent, restored half the cuts in public salaries, and canceled all the reduction in unemployment payments. He reduced the tax on automobiles and motorcycles by a quarter, a widespread boon; but the chief gift was to the income tax payer, who was allowed to keep over £20,000,000 in his pocket.

This first installment of reward for patience in suffering still leaves the British tax burden heavy beyond North American comprehension. Suppose you were a

[1] *Yorkshire Post*, February 24, 1932.
[2] This surplus was not due chiefly to recovery. It was due largely to the conversion of part of the national debt to lower interest rates, to a big payment of death duties on a large estate, to an increase in the yield from beer taxes, and to payment of only a token on the debt to America.

married man with one child. If you were a university head, your income tax on a salary of $10,000 in 1931 was $1,765; it is now reduced to $1,585, which is 15.8 per cent of your salary. If you were a university professor earning $5,000, you would have paid $640, but will now pay only $575, or 11.5 per cent of your salary. If you were a lecturer getting $2,500, you would now pay $125 (5 per cent) instead of $140. If you were a "big business executive," earning $50,000 a year, your income tax and surtax combined would now be a mere $17,425, or 35 per cent of your salary, instead of $19,360. If you were unmarried, your payments would be somewhat higher. Even a single artisan earning $1,000 a year pays $34 in income tax.

As with the income tax relief, so also with the other budget concessions. If you had a car, you would now pay only $3.75 per horsepower, instead of $5, but even that would cost you $26 a year on a "Baby Austin," and at least $100 on one of our "popular cars in the low-priced field," no matter what its age. There would still be a tax of sixteen cents a gallon on your gasoline; you could find no heavily taxed tobacco fit to smoke for less than twenty to tweny-five cents an ounce, and no good cigarettes cheaper than twelve cents for a packet of ten. If in spite of continued payment of such heavy taxes you still died a rich man, death duties would absorb a large slice of your estate: the death of a shipping magnate brought £8,000,000 to the Treasury last year, and provided the Chancellor with over a fifth of his surplus. The budget of 1934 allowed the taxpayers to keep £30,000,000; but it still takes £700,000,000 from them.

Of that sum, about half was swallowed up in payment of interest on the national debt. Relief from that interest load could come either by the terribly slow process of debt redemption through the sinking fund, or by a conversion of the debt to a lower rate of interest. The war had raised the interest level on all loans, for if gilt-edged borrowers paid 5 or 6 per cent, plain-edged ones must pay more, especially for long-term loans. A reduction of the rate on government bonds would consequently not merely lighten the burden of taxation, but would reduce the rate at which money could be borrowed, whether on mortgage, by the sale of corporation bonds, or in any other way. But a government which is drifting and incurring new debt instead of balancing its budget can do little to lower the rate on its old debt. Its credit rating is too poor.

The conversion of a war loan of £2,000,000,000 from 5 to 3½ per cent in the spring of 1932 was therefore a most important achievement. That loan was more than a quarter of the whole national debt, and the saving in interest was about £30,000,000. Later conversions of smaller sums followed, with new rates of 3 or 2½ per cent. The results were far-reaching. The Treasury needed far less money to meet its interest bills, and private borrowers benefited by the general reduction of interest rates on private long-term loans. Capital for building was now cheap enough to permit houses to be built in much greater numbers and with lighter interest burdens to be borne by the man who bought a house on installments or by the tenant who rented one. Building boomed. The average rate on new issues of industrial bonds fell about a quarter, and that on preferred stock about a fifth. By February, 1934, the *Economist* reported that British industry was "now beginning to reap the benefit of lower borrowing rates," and a stimulus was thus given to re-equipment and reorganization of plants and to the production of what we call "durable goods." Thus the conversion of national debt must rank as one of the most important recovery measures.

2. *Credit and Exchange Policy.* — When the financial crisis of 1931 was over, the government and the banks set out to pursue a policy that would provide cheap and abundant credit for the state and for private enterprise. The government placed an embargo on capital issues to foreign borrowers : this would prevent competition for loans from abroad and keep the supply of loanable capital at least equal to the demand. How far such an embargo was necessary is doubtful, since there were too many burned fingers in London as well as in New York, and few would have been willing to lend. Hence we have the strange fact that in 1932 not a single foreign capital issue was made in London, and that in 1933 only a million pounds were lent. In 1934 the embargo was lifted a little, by permitting countries that belonged to the "sterling group" to borrow for certain purposes. This group consisted of those dominions and foreign countries whose currencies were tied to sterling rather than to gold; it included Australia, New Zealand, India, and South Africa, as well as the Scandinavian countries and the Argentine. But loans to this group are still insignificant: the outflow of capital is still only a trickle.

The banks did their best to swell the supply of available credit. In 1932 the Bank of England reduced its bank rate from a high point of 6 per cent to 2 per cent, and has kept it at that point ever since. In addition it began to buy securities heavily, and the money it paid for them went to swell the resources on the basis of which the other banks could make loans. But borrowers were not forthcoming in numbers sufficient to take all the banks could offer. The business world was too prostrate or too nervous to use the available credit. When one of its members began to make a little progress and profit he often used the latter to repay some of the loan he had already obtained from the bank, and reviving businesses often financed the first stages of recovery out of their cash reserves instead of going to the banks.

In consequence bank loans actually fell heavily during 1932 and dropped still further the next year. Meanwhile funds rolled in from the United States during the months of bank panic, and from Holland, Belgium, and France when it seemed probable that these countries would be driven off gold. The British government in 1933 resorted less to short-term loans from the banks and borrowed from the general public on long-term at low rates. As a result the banks were glutted with funds. They could have extended an additional billion dollars worth of credit without crossing the danger line or disposing of any of their assets.

In such circumstances it seems incorrect to talk of "cheap money" as if it was the result of a deliberate policy steadily pursued by the banks of their own choice. To find uses for their funds they had to sell their services cheaply. Some of their resources they put into investments, and their competition with each other and with the ordinary buyer who was looking for a safe place for his money raised the price of good securities and reduced the consequent yield on the outlay. The rest they put out wherever a borrower could be found, at rates which scarcely gave a profitable return and which established "all time low" records.

Eventually the big banks united, went on strike, and refused to buy Treasury bills at less than one per cent discount, thus making their own code in defense against sweated wages. But chiselers soon appeared outside the union, offered smaller discounts, and forced a reduction of the code charges. Banking became in many respects so unremunerative that "sooner than seek out fresh business and fresh deposits [the banks] would rather see credit contract." [3] The country thus enjoyed a period of cheap credit partly from policy and partly from necessity. But cheap credit is of little use unless there is a borrower who can see his way to use it profitably, and if it is not used its ability to restore business or raise prices is nullified. If recovery continues, the demand for loans will doubtless grow and credit will cease to be cheap.

Great Britain has never been so deeply stirred by currency controversies as has the United States, and disputes about money have rarely got as far as the election platform. The political crisis of August, 1931, was caused in part by an attempt to keep on the gold standard, and the failure of the new government to keep what had been almost a pledge was ominous. There was dark reference to the *assignats* of the French Revolution, to the "conti-

[3] *Economist*, May 12, 1934.

nentals" of the American Revolution, to Russian rubles, Austrian crowns, and other paper currencies that had descended to worthlessness. Great play was made during the election with exhibits of worthless billion mark bills and of letters carrying fantastic values of stamps.

Fear that the pound would follow in the footsteps of these continental currencies was soon dispelled, and some people began to rejoice at the country's cleverness in having deserted gold, of having overthrown the golden calf, of having broken the golden fetters. What was the use of trying to work a gold standard when the conditions essential to its operation no longer existed? Not even a gold standard could stand on shifting foundations. "The economic consequences of Mr. Churchill" and his overvalued pound were now undone. The handicap to the export trade was removed: a depreciated pound — for sterling soon fell over 30 per cent in value against the dollar and franc — made British goods cheaper abroad and thus acted as a potential stimulus to exports. At the same time it made foreign goods dearer in England, thus acting as an automatic tariff. The country would export more, import less, and thus help to redress the adverse balance of payments.

In practice these boons and blessings were not by any means fully attained. Many other countries followed England away from gold; their currencies depreciated, and their goods did not become dearer in England nor did British goods become cheaper in their currencies. Japan's currency depreciated far more than did the pound, and she thus became a keener competitor than ever. Countries that remained on gold combated the cheap

British imports by raising their tariffs, by imposing anti-dumping duties, by making arbitrary valuations of British goods, or by applying quota restrictions to limit imports. When the United States depreciated its currency, the advantage the pound had enjoyed over the dollar soon vanished and was turned into a slight disadvantage. Any benefit that depreciation gave to exporters was therefore temporary and could easily be destroyed by counter-attack. Out of a battle in currency depreciation no one would emerge any better off in the long run, and a recent book on the devaluation of the pound [4] has suggested that the British action intensified the depression so greatly that it would have paid the French, American, and other central banks to have loaned Britain enough gold to keep her on the standard.

The chief benefit gained by leaving gold was probably unexpected. Most British onlookers in 1931 feared that imports would rise in price as the pound went down. But the price of those imports in terms of gold continued to fall till early in 1933, so that even a fallen pound bought as much of them as before. Hence there was no serious *rise* in the sterling cost of these goods. On the other hand there was no serious *fall* in the sterling cost of imports: the depreciation partly canceled out the fall in terms of gold. The sterling price of these imports, and of competing British produce, therefore remained comparatively stable. Producers and distributors had to face few and slight reductions in the price of their goods while prices were falling and spreading distress in gold countries. Internal purchasing power was therefore fairly well main-

[4] J. K. L. Clifford, *The Devaluation of the Pound* (1934).

tained where production was being carried on, and, supplemented by unemployment pay, this kept the ship on a fairly even keel.

This probably unexpected price stability and relief from the horrors of price deflation spread in a measure to those countries which left the gold standard as a result of Britain's departure. Their goods went far down in terms of gold, but dropped only a little in sterling. If they were debtors to England, they could pay their interest bills more easily, and buy more cheaply in the British market than in places where gold standards prevailed. Hence there gradually emerged what has become known as the sterling group. Sterling has not degenerated into a local currency; the sterling bill of exchange has been able to hold its own alongside bills drawn in currencies based on gold, and the paper pound seems to be slowly gaining the place once held by the old gold pound as a unit in international trade.

Escape from gold might have its benefits, but it had its costs, especially in the obstacle to external trade imposed by the fluctuating value of sterling. A cheaper pound might be good, but a widely or rapidly fluctuating pound was harmful. Those fluctuations were not now the result of variations in demand caused by ordinary commerce, but sprang from speculation in exchange and from the sudden international movements of short-term capital by owners seeking safety or profit in a world dominated by fear, rumor, and fits of nerves. A flight from the dollar would create a great demand for pounds and an increase in the value of sterling; a return to the dollar would cause a great selling of sterling and a consequent fall in its exchange value. To check these movements an Exchange Equalization Account was set up in April, 1932, with a fund of £150,000,000. This money was to be invested in securities or in gold in such manner as should seem best adapted for checking undue fluctuations in the exchange value of sterling.

Operations on the Account were naturally clouded in secrecy, but the verdict of an American student is that the trading was skillful and the operations successful.[5] Sudden fluctuations were fought, but no attempt was made to prevent "wide fluctuations . . . arising from major forces of a fundamental and national character."[6] The dollar and franc rates were kept from violent oscillation, but big long swings could not be prevented. When the United States left the gold standard and later established its exchange stabilization scheme the situation was changed, for now each of two countries was trying to keep its currency in steady relationship to something that was not steady. What part the operations have played in keeping the pound near to $5 or in keeping $5 near to £1 one cannot say; the main task of the British Account during the past year seems to have been to control the rate on Paris.

As an emergency protective expedient, the attempt to steady exchange rates has been necessary, and beneficial to trade. As an instrument of exchange control in normal times it would probably be unnecessary. Out of the chaos of the past three years there has emerged the ster-

[5] See the article on this subject by Alzada Comstock in *American Economic Review*, December, 1933.
[6] *Economist*, February 17, 1934.

ling group, the small bloc of countries still on gold, and the United States with a dollar whose vagaries have perhaps now come to an end. These three currency areas could find no basis for agreement at the World Economic Conference in 1933; they have all learned useful lessons since then, and agreement may be possible in the near future between at least two of them.

3. Trade Policy. — The most far-reaching changes in British policy came with the final abandonment of free trade and the adoption of a protective policy mitigated by imperial preference. In America depression has led many to doubt the efficacy of the traditional policy of high protection, and to recognize that "America must choose" whether she will shrink further within her shell and abandon exports, or open her ports a little wider in return for a heartier welcome of her wares in foreign parts. Since the passage of the Hawley-Smoot tariff the country has added fewer restrictions to overseas trade than any other nation, and the power given to the President to negotiate reciprocal treaties may mark the beginning of an era of greater liberalism in trade policy. In marked contrast, Britain has been led or driven in the opposite direction, and for three years has been engrossed in the work of erecting barriers round her harbors.

It is difficult for us in the large free trade area of the United States to realize the extent to which overseas produce has for nearly a century entered into British consumption. We may get a glimpse of it if we imagine each of the forty-eight states as a separate sovereign unit. Then Florida grapefruit, California peaches, Michigan cereals, and Pennsylvania coal become foreign imports to Minnesota. Texas cotton, woven into cloth in Massachusetts and made into shirts in New York, becomes a good example of international division of labor, as does a car built in Michigan with Pittsburgh steel made from Minnesota ore, shod with tires made in Ohio, lubricated with Texas oil and driven by California gasoline.

Yet that is only a pale reflection of cosmopolitanism, for the British housewife puts a girdle round the earth when she prepares a shopping list. The flour may have come from Australia or Canada, the butter from Denmark or New Zealand, the lamb from New Zealand or Australia, the beefsteak from the Argentine. The bacon may be Danish, the eggs Irish, the sugar German, the grapefruit may have come from Florida, the Levant, or the West Indies, the oranges from Spain, Australia, or South Africa, the apples from Tasmania, Nova Scotia, or British Columbia. So it is all through her house: the clothing is made of American cotton or Australian wool, the furniture of Baltic or Central American timber, the cutlery of steel manufactured from Swedish ore, while the crockery may have been made in Germany and bought at Woolworth's.

The British consumer did not therefore attach nationality to inanimate things. He rarely stopped to ask where an article had been produced; to him an apple was good not because it was British, Canadian, or Tasmanian, but because it was a good apple. He had what Mr. Fay has called a consumer's psychology, and wanted the greatest possible value for his money, regardless of national origins. Mr. Clay stated a common view when he said in 1931, "I feel no *moral* obligation to prefer some tariff commission's choice of the yarn my underclothing shall be made of to my own, and it would awaken in me no sense of sin if my bread contained less than the prescribed quota of British or dominion wheat."[7] At the height of the "Buy British" campaign a Yorkshire housewife — a lifelong Conservative — placed before us a dish of canned peaches. From their appearance they could have only one possible origin — California. Asked if they were of British or dominion growth, she replied, "I don't know, but I do know they are the best I can get." The empty can was fetched for examination. It bore the name of a well-known American brand, but our hostess was defiantly unrepentant.

If national or imperial salvation depended on making purchases patriotic, the task was a big one. During the fall of 1931 the "Buy British" campaign was waged intensely, with stickers, billboards, window displays, and radio appeals. One high spot in the crusade was the christening of a ship with a bottle of Scotch whisky instead of with a bottle of foreign wine. The campaign probably had some effect, as had the Empire Marketing Board's work: in the presence of national danger even buyers may become nationalistic. But when a New Zealand economist found a Lancashire shoe factory stamping its wares with "Foreign made" or some such label and asked for an explanation, the reply was that customers had grown suspicious of the quality of British goods, since such urgent appeals were necessary to sell them. Our own appeals to "Buy American" — printed on paper

[7] *The World's Economic Crisis and the Way of Escape* (1932), p. 157.

made from Canadian wood — were a fitting counterpart to the British campaign.

A protective tariff was the next step. This was not a triumph for propaganda, the result of any intellectual conversion, or a response to orders from the electorate. Most academic economists were free traders even at the worst of the crisis: they regarded a tariff as a worse cure for a bad disease, and pointed out that the depreciation of the pound had given the local producer both protection and an export bounty. Free trade died of economic factitis and the luck of politics. The luck was that of the Conservatives, who, thanks to their overwhelming weight in the National party, were able to make national salvation and protection synonymous. The Labor flight killed free trade just as the potato blight killed the Corn Laws in 1846.

The pressure of economic facts was with the tariff advocates. The closing of foreign markets by panic-stricken or nationalistic policies curtailed British exports, and the invisible exports were visibly shrinking. At the same time Britain was almost the only open market into which other countries could easily get their goods. The amount of distress dumping of manufactures on British wharves cannot be measured, but almost every manufacturer could quote instances of goods which had come in from Poland, Germany, Czechoslovakia, America, and elsewhere, and which were being offered at very low prices. The farmer's plight was almost as bad as that of the factory owner. British exports fell by half during a period when imports dropped only a third; the visible imports in 1931 were more than double the visible exports, and the balance of payments showed a frightful deficit.

To cope with the situation, check abnormal imports, and meet the clamor for action, temporary protection was given to several products in November, 1931, and in February, 1932, the real tariff was imposed. Its aims were seven in number: (1) to correct the balance of payments; (2) to fortify the national finances by raising fresh revenue by methods which will put no undue burden on any section of the community; (3) to insure against a rise in the cost of living such as might follow from an unchecked depreciation of the currency; (4) "by a system of moderate protection, scientifically adjusted to the needs of agriculture, to transfer to our own factories and our own fields work which is now done elsewhere," thus decreasing unemployment; (5) by judicious use of protection "to enable and encourage our people to render their methods of production and distribution more efficient"; (6) "to arm ourselves with an instrument" for negotiation "with foreign countries which have not hitherto paid very much attention to our suggestions" and for use where discrimination is made against British goods; and (7) to offer advantages "to the countries of the Empire in return for advantages which they now give or in the near future may be disposed to give us."[8]

These seven aims were sought through four main provisions. (1) A 10 per cent tariff was imposed on all imports except those subject already to duties or included

[8] The words quoted are those used by Mr. Neville Chamberlain in introducing the tariff, February 4, 1932.

in a free list. The free list included little beyond food and raw materials, and not all foods were on it. (2) An independent Imports Advisory Committee was set up, with power to recommend increased duties or the removal of articles from the free list. (3) Preference in the form of exemption from the new duties was granted to dominion products until after the Ottawa Imperial Conference. (4) The Treasury was given power to raise duties to 100 per cent on imports from countries which discriminated against British goods, and to lower or remove them on goods from countries with which reciprocal trade agreements were made.

When the Corn Laws were repealed in 1846 bells were rung and flags were flown; bonfires burned and processions marched through the streets of industrial towns. When free trade was killed not a drum was heard, not a funeral note: there were no popular demonstrations, and no flags were unfurled — even at half-mast. The general disposition was to "wait and see" what happened. Some good might be done, some jobs might be forthcoming as imports were checked, and the new port might prove a safe haven in the storm. How the export industries were to be helped was not quite clear, except perhaps by gaining easier access to imperial markets and by reciprocal bargains which would lower foreign tariff walls. The tariff and the free list were admittedly rough and ready expedients: the rates were too high to please some producers and too low to satisfy others, and the free list was criticized for what it included or excluded.

During the past two and a half years the seven purposes have all been pursued. The tariff committee has made recommendations, and many duties are much higher than the general 10 per cent level; the Ottawa Conference did its work in the middle of 1932 and imperial preference is now widespread; there has been some experience of retaliation, and some effort at reciprocity. What are the results?

In the first place there was a quick decline in the value and volume of imported manufactures and in the adverse balance. The depreciation of the pound, the decline in prices, the continuance of the depression, and the imposition of the tariff combined to reduce the imports of manufactures by over £100,000,000 in 1932, and by a further £7,000,000 in 1933. But there the decline ended, and in 1934 there has been an increase in the imports of consumers' factory products and also of those manufactured or partly manufactured articles which are the raw material of some British industries, e. g., metals, iron and steel products, and chemicals. Total imports did not fall nearly so heavily as did those of manufactured wares, and of the increase in imports since recovery began the greater part has been in raw materials and foodstuffs. Meanwhile exports of British goods declined by only £24,000,000 in 1932, rose a little in 1933, and in the first half of 1934 climbed £11,000,000 above those for the same part of 1933.

A tentative conclusion can therefore be drawn that the combination of tariff, depreciation, and other factors checked the inrush of goods, gave such harassed industries as iron and steel a chance to regain their breath, and transferred a slice of the market from the foreign to the domestic producer. The country thus discovered that "in the crisis home production can be largely maintained by the displacement of imports."[9] But recovery has caused an increased demand for many of those semi-manufactured or manufactured imports in the production of which the external producer has a competitive advantage.

The reduction of imports reacted on the balance of payments, for the excess of commodity imports was heavily reduced, and when the Board of Trade worked out its balance sheet it found that the adverse balance of £104,000,000 had shrunk to £4,000,000 in 1933. Thus, as the *Manchester Guardian* put it, "viewed as a whole the country is now spending on what the rest of the world has to sell just the equivalent of its own receipts from new sales of its own goods and services, and from interest upon old reserves (excluding capital payments)."[10]

In the second place, imperial economic relations have been brought down from the clouds of after-dinner rhetoric to earth. When the delegates gathered in Ottawa in July, 1932, Britain was in a position such as she had never occupied in her free trade days. She had granted preference or freedom from duty in her tariff schedules since 1919; she had exempted the dominions from the duties imposed in 1931-1932, and was now in a position to offer still more substantial benefits. But whereas past preferences granted by the dominions or by Britain had been unconditional tokens of imperial kinship, they were now to be the result of businesslike bargains.

[9] *New Statesman*, August 25, 1934.
[10] *Manchester Guardian Weekly*, March 2, 1934.

Some people resented the very thought of bargaining round the family table. The Federation of British Industries frowned on any suggestion of haggling, preferred "an atmosphere of mutual accommodation and readiness on the part of all to make the maximum possible contribution toward conjoint Empire interests," and suggested as a guiding rule a policy of "complementary industrial production." [11] Let each unit be satisfied to do chiefly those things it could do best.

Other groups used less honeyed words. A committee of the National Farmers Union said preference should start with a 10 per cent tariff on dominion produce rather than free entry. Northern clothmakers said bluntly that "some of the dominions will have to adopt a vastly different attitude toward the Mother Country" since even their preferential rates were so high that it was "virtually impossible to import goods into those countries." [12] The crucial question was not how much lower the preferred rate was than the rate on foreign goods, but how high the preferred rate was. It was little consolation to know that an American was drowning in a hundred feet of water if the Englishman was drowning in fifty.

For the British delegates Ottawa was a summer school in imperial economics, in which they learned the folly of talk about Empire free trade, the strength of dominion protectionist sentiment, and the plain speaking that postwar adolescents use in arguing with a parent. To the British hint that imperial trade be fostered by reducing duties within the family, the dominions retorted with

[11] Memorandum published in *Yorkshire Post*, May 6, 1932.
[12] *Yorkshire Post*, February 12, 1932.

the alternative suggestion that duties on goods from outside be raised instead.

The conflict of interests was seen especially in discussions between Britain and Canada, for Canada is the most industrialized of the dominions, her manufacturers are powerfully organized and skilled in the exertion of pressure, and the conference was held in Canada. Australia also has fairly well-developed industries, a powerful manufacturers' organization, and a wage-earning class wedded to high protection. That these dominions should take layers off their tariff walls for the benefit of British iron, steel, textile, or shoe producers was not to be expected, and the British had not reached the stage where they dare use the threat of duties on dominion foodstuffs or of reciprocal pacts with foreign primary producers as a talking point.

The final outcome of the conference was a number of agreements, some of which were to run for five years. In them Great Britain continued the existing preferences, which otherwise would have expired in November, 1932, agreed to increase duties on some foreign foodstuffs, and added some new ones, especially a small one on wheat. She agreed to prohibit imports of goods which any foreign state was dumping into Britain at prices which "frustrated" the preference to dominion producers. The foreign state meant Russia, whose political, economic, and religious color was intensely disliked by the Canadian government, and whose lumber was said to be competing unfairly with that of Canada. Finally, Britain promised that if she had to take steps to protect her farmers by tariffs or quotas, she would do nothing to impair dominion exports of meats till 1934 or of poultry and dairy products till 1935.

In return the dominions undertook to increase the preference on some British goods. They also agreed to allow British producers to appeal to their tariff boards for a revision of duties. In the light of recommendations made by the tariff board after hearing British and dominion manufacturers, rates would be adjusted in order to give British exporters "full opportunity of reasonable competition on the basis of the relative cost of economical and efficient production." The tariff would be a fair handicap to the British producer: it would not bar him from the race.

These agreements have now run for two years; they have raised interesting problems and roused some dissatisfaction. The Federation of British Industries says, "They have proved more beneficial to the dominions than to Great Britain," and considers the time "premature" to express an opinion concerning their contribution to trade revival. In reply, dominion manufacturers point to the keener competition they are experiencing from British rivals, as seen, for example, in the doubled importation of Lancashire cottons into Canada between the first half of 1933 and that of 1934.

From the statistical evidence available up to the middle of 1934 some conclusions can be drawn. Empire sales to Britain and purchases from her held their own and even increased slightly in 1933, during a period when trade with other parts of the world was slumping badly. From this statement the Irish Free State must be excluded, for the trade war between London and Dublin cut the trade each way by more than two-fifths. In 1934 trade between Britain and the rest of the Empire has grown a little more rapidly than that with the rest of the world. The growth of Britain's imperial purchases has been more rapid than that of her sales, and while the overseas producers are securing an increasing share of the British import trade they are not taking an increasing fraction of British exports, for the portion has remained almost unchanged at just over two-fifths since 1929.

These generalizations, based on totals, need to be broken up, and when this is done unpleasant patches, such as the trade across the Irish Sea, are counterbalanced by happier conditions in other areas. Thus Canada's trade returns for 1933–1934 show that a combination of recovery and of Ottawa has expanded substantially her trade with the rest of the Empire. In that year her sales to Britain and her purchases from that country rose about a quarter. Britain bought nearly half of Canada's exports, against three-tenths in 1929; Britain supplied nearly a quarter of her imports, against 15 per cent in 1929. Her trade, outward and inward, with other dominions had expanded. In a small Canadian town one can now see British movies and buy New Zealand apples, Australian canned fruit, and South African oranges. Four years ago not one of these imports would have been encountered; they are indications of the slowly growing interchange of goods between the different parts of the Commonwealth, and in the case of Canada they represent in large part a decline in relative importance of the United States both as buyer and as seller.

The complaint that Britain has benefited less, and

more slowly, than the dominions is well-grounded. The concessions she made were immediate, and strengthened the grip the dominions already had on British food and raw material markets. The concessions to her depended largely on tariff adjustments; some tariff changes were included in the agreements, but in making others the dominion governments were to be guided by their tariff boards and had to consider the reaction on industrial opinion in their electorates as well as the effect on their customs receipts. Movement, if it came at all, would certainly be slow and small. In days of depression a lowering of tariffs looks like suicide.

In Canada British manufacturers of woolens and of shoes have brought cases before the Tariff Board and attempts have been made to compare the costs of production in England and Canada. The first attempt broke down because it could find no basis of comparison; the second decided that the existing tariff rate was fair. Some arbitrary valuations, made by the customs officers during the years when the pound was at a discount in terms of Canadian dollars, have been removed; but the status of the Tariff Board and its power to do much have been upset by a Supreme Court decision. Thus two years after Ottawa the old tariff stands little changed.

In Australia some reduction has taken place in the charges on British goods; but the application of the competitive principle, by which the tariff was to cover the difference in costs of production, underwent a strange revision in 1934, when the duty on certain cotton goods was raised in order to take account of the higher cost of Australian-grown raw cotton. In New Zealand, the least industrialized dominion and also the one most dependent on Britain for its market, the tariff was revised in 1934, and some very large reductions were made in the rates on British goods. But by that time, as we shall see later, the tariff problem was taking on a different hue. In short, two years have dispelled any hope that Ottawa would shower blessings on British industries, and a recent campaign in Lancashire for the boycott of Australian produce in retaliation for the increased duty on cotton goods strikes a new note in imperial sentiment.

If British exporters have been disappointed at the slow arrival of tariff concessions, some dominion exporters have been disturbed by the development of the new commercial policy in England, for British producers rapidly developed a belief that imperialism begins at home, and customs officials have become suspicious of goods that claimed preference. How could they be sure that Canadian wheat coming from an American port was really Canadian? How could they discover whether an article stamped "Made in Canada" contained a sufficient amount of Canadian material and labor—say 50 per cent—to permit it to pass in free or at the preferred rate? Might it not be an American product that had merely been assembled or finished in a Canadian branch factory?

In 1933 two British officials were in Canada examining the extent to which Canadian cars were Canadian, and of three automobile firms that claimed the preferred rate only one was granted it. But, said British car makers, if 50 per cent Empire content is demanded, why not 75 per cent? This question was asked with increasing urgency when in 1934 the new American car designs and the reduction of the British tax on engine power threatened British automobile builders with an invasion of the home and overseas markets. The customs officials again went to Canada, and requests for a higher "Empire content" seem inevitable. As the Canadian motor industry still depends in some measure on imported parts, the result on its export trade may be serious.

A second cause of anxiety came to Canada in the operation of the lumber agreement, by which an embargo was to be placed on Russian exports of timber to England if the preference was being frustrated "through state action" — but Canada had to prove the frustration. Canada's natural lumber market is the United States, and Britain's natural source of supply is the Baltic. But Canadian access to the American market was narrowed by the slump in building after 1929 and by a tariff war between Ottawa and Washington, and Canadian interests therefore sought the British market more eagerly. The building boom of 1933 caused a great expansion of British lumber imports, of which Russia supplied the largest part. The Canadian woodmen endeavored to cut Russia out by urging their government to claim an embargo, and the British authorities asked the importing companies and the Soviet government for their comments on this claim.

The argument that followed was full and frank. The importers praised the superior quality of Russian wood and said some other Baltic country would get the business if Russia did not. The Canadians criticized Russia's selling methods and talked about the preservation of Canadian rights under the Ottawa agreement. The result was that no embargo was declared, that Russian supplies rose, that Canadian deliveries did likewise, and that the Quebec Forests Products Commission asked the dominion government to "secure observance of treaties drawn up between Canada and Great Britain" — a difficult task for a government which had done so little to fulfill the promises of tariff adjustment.

Only the most optimistic and ill-informed imperialists believed that trade agreements would achieve great results or work without friction. The vested interests of manufacturers and the strongly protectionist views of labor in the two largest dominions were too powerful to make any far-reaching concessions to British exporters possible, especially in the depths of a depression. At the same time there was in dominion circles no fear that the open door through which their exports had been free to pour would ever be even partly closed to them. They lived in the best of all possible empires. But they made one mistake: they forgot the British farmer. They were not alone in that forgetfulness, for in Britain also he was "the forgotten man." But when he was rediscovered, strange clouds began to appear in the imperial sky.

CHAPTER FIVE

THE REDISCOVERY OF THE FARMER

FREE TRADE LEFT ALL FORMS OF ENTERPRISE — AGRICUL-
ture, industry, mining, and shipping — to work out their
own salvation. When it was first enthroned as a policy
that work was easy, even for the farmer, since the agricultural exploitation of the new world and the development of cheap ocean transport had scarcely begun in
earnest. But the golden age of English agriculture came
to an end in the seventies, when the flood of cheap grain,
meat, and dairy produce began to flow in from Russia
and the distant continents.

Continental farmers met this invasion from the new
world by securing protection or by turning to new products, e. g., butter and bacon in Denmark. British farmers
got no protection; there were not enough of them to
exercise political pressure as did the swarms of peasant
proprietors on the continent. They did, however, as the
decades went by, obtain concessions of various kinds,
and Dr. Venn, a leading British agricultural economist,
calculated in 1933 that direct grants, relief from central
and local taxation, and indirect assistance comprised a
total public aid to agriculture of over £45,000,000 a
year. Slowly and painfully they cut their costs, changed
their production programs, and specialized on goods
which met with less intense external competition, such as
high-grade meats, milk, dairy produce, poultry, fruit,
and vegetables.

Pre-war British agriculture supplied the market with only about one-fifth of its wheat and about half its meat. According to one estimate, the country produced about £170,000,000 of the foodstuffs it needed and imported £200,000,000. To supply these imports twenty million acres of land were said to be employed growing wheat, and a similar area was supplying meat and dairy produce. Most of the exports of Australia, New Zealand, and Canadian farms went to Great Britain, as did 95 per cent of Denmark's butter and the larger part of the Argentine's beef and of Ireland's dairy and hog products. Virtually the whole of the world's exports of bacon, mutton, and lamb went to supply the British larder.

Protection for the British farmer was obviously no simple task. A tariff on food would have to be paid on over half the country's supply, and history showed that parties which went to the electors with plans to "tax the people's food" fared ill. A tariff that exempted dominion supplies would still leave the British farmer exposed to serious competitors. A tariff on dominion supplies and a higher one on foreign would be unpopular in the dominions, while the exclusion of produce from countries that had their main market in Britain might have serious repercussions on the sale of British manufactures in those regions. Restrictions on food imports would prevent foreigners from paying for "invisible exports," and especially from making their interest payments. In short, protection to the British farmer meant a challenge to many integral parts of the economy which the preceding century had designed.

Yet something must be done, for the farmers in 1931

found their tongues and wanted higher prices. If the factory was to be sheltered, so must be the farm, and with it the country home of the landlord. British agriculture is not in the hands of small peasant proprietors, but is conducted on medium or large farms, with the aid of some hired help, by farmers who rent their holdings from comparatively large landowners. The farmer votes Conservative, as do most landlords. Hence the triumph of the National party, dominated by its Conservative element, meant that when landlords and farmers spoke they would receive an attentive hearing.

Some of them had already been heard, and forty thousand farmers were being helped by the grant of a heavy subsidy, established in 1925, on sugar beets. This subsidy, plus various rebates and drawbacks, has cost the Exchequer £40,000,000 in nine years. It has caused such a great expansion in production that the country now imports only three-fourths of its supply instead of all of it; it has added to the existing chaos and world overproduction, and injured the West Indian colonial producers. The British consumer pays a high price for this "selective and enormously expensive favour to one section of agriculture," [1] and when the time comes for the subsidy to expire the vested interest of growers and refiners will prove again that no country can touch sugar without getting its fingers permanently sticky.

A bounty is one alternative to a protective tariff, a quota is a second, and the chief effect of the depression on European commercial policy has been the application of the quota principle in one form or another. A quota

[1] *Times Weekly Edition*, January 11, 1934.

may limit imports in order to give the local producer the rest of the market, without any limit to the amount he can try to sell. The British wheat quota of 1932 turned this plan around, by giving the wheat-grower an assured part of the market, and then leaving importers to sell as much as they could. In addition, it gave him an assured price. Its aim was, in the official language of its sponsor, "to provide wheat-growers with a secure market and an enhanced price for home-grown wheat of millable quality, without a subsidy from the Exchequer and without encouraging the extension of wheat cultivation to land unsuitable for the crop."

The secure market was to be provided by announcing each August the amount of British wheat that could benefit from the plan during the next year; the extension of cultivation was to be checked by limiting this amount to 48,000,000 bushels. On this "anticipated supply" the farmer was to receive the market price, but if that price was less than 45/— a quarter (about $1.35 a bushel) he was to receive a "deficiency payment" which would lift his total income to 45/— a quarter. The money for these payments was to be obtained by a levy on flour millers or importers, according to the quantity of flour they handled; the millers passed the levy on in the form of higher flour prices. Thus the consumer paid the miller, the miller paid the Wheat Fund, and the Fund paid the farmer.

When this plan was introduced farmers were receiving about 25/— a quarter for wheat, and the subsidy was therefore 20/—, a substantial gift. They were producing about half the 48,000,000 bushels fixed as a maximum. There was much room for expansion. In two years — years when the great wheat-producing countries were striving to get rid of the wheat glut by curtailing acreage and limiting exports — the British acreage rose more than a third. But the area is still far below that of 1914, and if farmers reach the maximum production permitted, the country will still depend on the outside world for three-fourths of its wheat supply. Wheat will remain a minor part of British agriculture.

What then of the major part, the production of meats, milk, vegetables, dairy and poultry produce, and other commodities, which comprise over two-thirds of the value of goods sent to market? Some of these commodities, especially milk and potatoes, face no competition from without, but the others do. In 1930 the home production of beef was a little less than the imports, but that of mutton and lamb was much less. As a rough generalization one might say that those who could afford British meats and dairy produce bought them, while poorer people bought chilled beef from the Argentine, frozen beef and mutton from New Zealand or Australia, and imported bacon and dairy products. The British article was usually dearer than the imported, and the difference was not all explained in terms of quality.

Foreign supplies of fruit, vegetables, bacon, and dairy produce were subjected to a tariff; but the country's dependence on meat imports was too large to permit the imposition of duties. Even when the "Buy British" campaign was at its height the government refused to feed the army and navy on native meat. The roast beef of Old England was not for Tommies and Tars. The stock-

raisers were intensely disappointed when they learned
that meat was on the free list, but their turn came eventually, as part of an agricultural policy which embraced
import quotas, marketing schemes, and subsidies, in addition to the tariffs already imposed on many commodities.

The development of this policy is probably the most
unexpected part of recent British history. It is a composite outcome of ideas on cooperative marketing which
had emerged before 1931, of the fall in farm prices, and
of the energetic personality of Mr. Walter Elliot, minister of agriculture since late 1932.

Mr. Elliot may be called the Wallace of British agricultural policy, and already a new noun — Elliotism —
has passed into currency. His views of the farm problem
lead him to a far-reaching program of controlled marketing, with quotas regulating the amount of produce
that flows in from outside, and with marketing organization to handle or control distribution. "On a scarcity
market," he says, "feed it with all you've got. You don't
need to organize for that. . . . On a glutted market you
have to feed into the saw only what the saw will cut.
You have to supply only what the market will stand.
That means restriction of supply." [2] Restriction can
come either "by conscious regulation or by the producers going broke and out of business" in the old-
fashioned way of laissez faire.

The British position is that of a glutted market, and
of a farming class which has suffered because the national
policy has for long been one of buying all over the world
in the cheapest market. The new deal in England means

[2] Interview in *New York Times*, July 8, 1934.

that "in these islands we intend to ensure that British agriculture shall continue to thrive, and if we can ensure it, to flourish." That attitude calls for the acceptance of three postulates: (1) "We cannot expect any vast increase in the consumption of food. (2) Apart from any increase in consumption, home production can be increased only at the cost of lower imports. (3) British farmers, however efficient, cannot cope with the importation of job lots of food at knockout prices." [3] "The average man here, producing the average crops, cannot compete, and never could, with the selected man producing the selected crop at the selected moment. . . . Hence you must insulate the average man." [4]

Insulation does not mean isolation, or any attempt to give the British farmer a monopoly of the home market. The country cannot feed itself; it must always import much food if it is to sell goods abroad; and an agricultural policy cannot be pushed ahead regardless of the reaction on export industries. But there must be a better balance between town and country, and this can be attained only when agriculture takes a larger place in national life and policy than it has done for three generations.

Even today, Mr. Elliot points out, it is far from being a minor industry. There are more people gainfully engaged in agriculture than in coal mining. There are as many as in the whole of the textile industries plus all the men making or repairing motor cars and motorcycles. If the purchasing power of that big block of consumers

[3] *Times Weekly Edition*, November 30, 1933.
[4] *New York Times*, July 8, 1934.

fails, the nation is hard hit. There is as much capital sunk in agriculture as in all the British investments in Europe and South America put together, or in Australia, New Zealand, India, and Ceylon combined. "These are the figures which make it necessary for us to say on every occasion that unless we succeed in reviving agriculture we cannot hope to have a prosperous Britain." This viewpoint is common in America, but it has not been urged by men in high places in England for many a long day.

The way to insulation, balance, and a smiling countryside lay through import quotas to prevent the glutting of the market, marketing schemes, subsidies, and better farming. At Ottawa the British delegates promised to limit foreign imports of meat. They would take 1931–1932 as the base year, and either fix the imports of that year as the quota, thus preventing an increase in future supplies, or reduce the quantity by stages during the next two years. This would prevent the foreigner from increasing his exports to Britain, or gradually reduce them. The dominions were guaranteed free and unregulated entry for their meats till June, 1934, and for their poultry and dairy produce till 1935. But it was understood by a gentleman's agreement that they would cooperate without compulsion and limit their meat exports, keeping them at or near those of 1931–1932.

The British government then turned to foreign countries, and in trade agreements made with Denmark, Argentina, and other countries quotas were laid down and provisions for their imposition or alteration were agreed on. In the case of Denmark, imports of her staple exports were to be duty-free or subject to a limited duty, but a quota might be applied to them "in so far as may be necessary to secure the effective operation of a scheme or schemes for the regulation of the marketing of domestic supplies of these products." This proviso was included in most of the other trade agreements.

With the Argentine, agreement was reached in a treaty of 1933; a progressive reduction of frozen meats to two-thirds the level of the base year was to be made, but the main export — that of chilled beef — was not to be reduced "unless it appeared necessary to secure a remunerative level of prices in the United Kingdom market," and if any serious cut was found desirable a similar reduction must be made in supplies from the dominions.

Once started, the policy of "quantitative regulation" gathered speed quickly. Under marketing schemes it was applied to bacon and butter. It could be imposed on foreign countries within the terms and limits of the trade agreements, and dominions were urged to "voluntary limitation." The *Times Weekly Edition* of December 28, 1933, reported that "Canada has wisely and generously agreed to the same voluntary limitation (of beef exports) as last year, and has thus avoided a statutory order affecting imports from Canada." But the Irish Free State, which was engaged in a trade war with Britain, had its quota reduced by half in early 1934. Denmark saw its bacon exports to Britain scaled down, and when the New Zealand Dairy Board refused to accept voluntarily a limit on its butter and cheese exports, there was much plain speech in London, and the New Zealand government had to calm the waters by assuming full responsibility for the dairy industry.

The British market, once an open door to foreign and imperial farm produce, is thus being closed, not merely by a tariff which may be jumped by goods that can find no other market but by a statistical veto. It is being converted into a turnstile, which revolves a definite number of times and is then locked. At the moment interest centers on beef imports. The Argentine agreement runs till 1936, but the Ottawa beef pacts expired in June, 1934. The way was therefore partly open for a new policy. In April a Reorganisation Commission for Fat Stock issued its report, recommending control of all imports of meats of all kinds and from all quarters; but if regulation of imports and of marketing failed to restore British meat to a remunerative price, a levy, similar to that made on flour, should be imposed on all imported supplies.

Armed with this report the government entered into discussion with the dominions "with a view to finding some system of reducing their meat imports into the United Kingdom that would be accepted voluntarily" by them. The discussion proving fruitless, the British authorities adopted a temporary policy of subsidizing native stock-raisers to the extent of £3,000,000 during the next six months. But they made it quite clear that reduced imports and a levy were the essentials of their long-run plan. In 1935 the agreements dealing with dairy produce expire, and further restriction on their importation may come then.

Restriction and reduction of imports are only part of the new agricultural policy. There must be organized marketing as well. British farmers have been slow to cooperate for the processing and sale of their produce.

Grading and standardization have received little attention, and the farmer has suffered in competition with the thoroughly standardized supplies from overseas. There has been lack of harmony between supplies and market requirements, whether as to quantity and quality or in terms of time and place.

The Labor government in 1931 tried to help farmers in its Agricultural Marketing Act. With the consent of a majority of producers of a commodity, a marketing scheme could be set up. At its head would be a board, which would undertake the sale of the commodity or regulate the price at which it could be sold and the kinds, grades, and varieties that might be sold. Its rule extended over any minority of producers who had not approved of the scheme. The National government expanded the plan by giving power to control the quantity to be sold as well as the price, and by conferring on the Board of Trade authority to limit the quantity of imports where a marketing scheme was in operation or was being planned.

Marketing boards are already at work dealing with hops, potatoes, hogs, bacon, and milk. They have under their control about two-fifths of the total value of the livestock and crop output of the country, and plans for sugar, meat, eggs, and poultry are under consideration. Like most agricultural schemes they are complicated. A plan may be prepared by the producers or by a reorganization commission; it must be approved by parliament and accepted by two-thirds of the producers. The board licenses producers and fixes prices or actually sells the product, and the government controls imports. The board may estimate the demand for a commodity and allot a quota to each producer or make a contract to take from him a stated quantity of produce. The potato planter who exceeds his allotted acreage can be fined.

Behind the board is the authority of the state, and also sometimes the purse. In the milk marketing plan the government is subsidizing for two years all milk delivered to dairy factories, in order to guarantee a minimum price and keep the milk from flowing into the "liquid market" where prices are higher. To clean up the dairy herds it is spending £750,000 during the next few years, while a publicity fund, provided half by the state and half by the producers, is to be used to stimulate consumption of milk and dairy produce.

The pattern of the "new cooperation" has become rapidly and clearly defined, and may be extended to the production and marketing of still more commodities. A recent examination of the herring industry found surplus capacity, glutted markets, cutthroat competition, weak selling organization, and financial statements written in red ink. The remedy proposed was "an overriding authority and a basic structure," with a board at its head. Boats were to be licensed, and the number of them was to be reduced by refusing licenses to the less seaworthy. Since the industry could not afford to bear the load of a levy with which to compensate the owners of discarded boats, let the Treasury grant £50,000 for that purpose and make loans for the provision of a smaller number of better boats. The board would control sales and act as agent for the export trade. Eventually a levy might be imposed, but at first the state must subsidize.

In commenting on this proposal one critic surveyed the field of controlled and subsidized marketing as follows: "So the Briton will add licensed milk and subsidized sugar to his morning cup of tea, taking his breakfast from a quota of bacon, a restricted egg, or a licensed kipper. He eats the bread of deficiency payments, but, alas, his marmalade is the un-English and unlimited orange. His lunch and dinner make up for that lacuna; his beef is sauced with subsidy, his potatoes are served schemed, levied, and marketed." [5]

Looking back on the early results of these varied agricultural policies Mr. Elliot last June claimed that the tide had turned for British agriculture. The acreages under wheat, barley, and vegetables had expanded. Imports of canned milk had fallen heavily, while the exports had doubled. Egg production had mounted, and in Lancashire there were "more hens than people." The hog industry had grown rapidly and it was difficult to "deal with the droves upon droves, the hundreds of thousands of pigs which are rushing and squealing upon us from every part. . . . As soon as it even looked like a profitable proposition to produce pigs in this country bacon pig production expanded 70 per cent in a few months" — a remark which suggests that disorder does not vanish when foreign supplies are reduced. The country had become almost self-sufficing in fruit and vegetables, and recent remarkable improvements in canning had expanded the demand for these products. Prices of farm produce had risen a little, and the wages and hours of three hundred thousand farm workers had been improved. "There

[5] *Manchester Guardian Commercial*, August 25, 1934.

is no justification for any foolish optimism," said Mr. Elliot, but the tide had turned, and "the cultivation of the land will become more important as time goes on."

A recent dispassionate survey of the marketing schemes reveals that control has raised the price of hops, but has had no marked effect as yet on the price of potatoes. Milk marketing, "if it has not raised prices, has at least maintained them." The hog scheme "so far has had little effect on home bacon pig prices, but has led to an increase in production, partly owing to oversanguine expectation on the part of producers, but partly by offering greater stability and by stimulating higher quality production." The main effect of restricting Danish imports was to raise the price of Danish bacon while that of British was falling, since bacon eaters brought up on "Danish streaky" refused to be patriotic or turn to the local product. In general, experience seems to have shown that the farmer's hope of higher prices has been checked by the low level of consumers' incomes in consequence of the depression. If and when those incomes rise it may be possible for their recipients to pay higher prices for farm produce; otherwise an increase in the farmer's return must come from better grading and from economies in distribution. But the marketing schemes do not attempt to do away with the existing channels of distribution, and it is highly doubtful whether producers will be able "to increase their price much at the expense of the middleman." [6]

The wider long-run effects of this attempt to foster

[6] See Ruth Cohen, "Agricultural Reorganization and Price Control," *Economic Journal*, September, 1934.

agriculture can only be guessed. No one questions the value of agricultural cooperation, or even of the attempt to make it watertight by imposing the will of the majority on all producers. But there is some truth in the contention of the *Economist* that none of the marketing boards has shown much willingness of its own initiative to increase the efficiency of the industry. "In the last thirty months farmers have been given selling monopolies and import restrictions, but they still demand special subsidies before any *quid pro quo* in the way of reorganization or improved efficiency is forthcoming." [7] Subsidies given as small temporary aids may become large parts of the permanent income of the industry if a sufficient number of persons receive them to build up a strong vested interest; they may become old soldiers who never die.

The possibility of conflict between agriculture and the rest of a highly industrialized country is real, and the safeguards provided for the protection of consumers are flimsy. Only 7 per cent of the British population depends directly on agriculture for its livelihood. It is a big enough minority to receive consideration in days when the state is the friend of all classes, but it is small enough to be expected to recognize the interests of the other 93 per cent. Mr. Elliot at times sees the danger ahead if the agricultural class gets all that some of its spokesmen demand. "If you cut down the importations into this country you must also cut down exportations from this country." Hence "we [agriculturists] should not blind

[7] See three articles on "Our Agricultural Policy" in the *Economist*, July 28, August 4, 11, 1934.

ourselves to the interests of industry as the industrialists of the nineteenth century blinded themselves to the interests of agriculture." But he admits it is hard for even a cabinet minister to keep his vision clear, and it is much harder for the farmer — in every country.

The interests of the towns and of industry are not the only ones that may be threatened, for the new deal to agriculture has brought anxiety to the dominions. Their primary producers fear a steadily declining, or at best a stationary, British market for some of their staple exports, and wonder how far the decrease may go. For generations they have worked on the assumption that however much they increased their output there was a ready market waiting to absorb their goods. Now all that is changing. They have already had some taste of what happens under "quantitative regulation." In July, 1934, the secretary of the Western Canadian Stock Growers Association said the British plan to regulate cattle imports was a "grievous blow to the cattle industry in Western Canada." In the following month an Alberta cabinet minister went to Ottawa to suggest that the Dominion government share with the packers and the Alberta government the cost of buying at fifty cents a hundredweight, of killing, and of turning into desiccated hogs' food seventy-five thousand head of cattle for which there was no fodder in Alberta and no market in Britain.

In New Zealand the prospect of restricted British markets has caused much heart searching. The depreciation of her exchange to four-fifths the value of sterling gave her exporters an advantage in the British market, and as their deliveries of meats and dairy produce in the London market had increased substantially since the onset of the depression the charge was made that they were practicing exchange dumping. When quotas came over the horizon, many farmers began to wonder if the free market could be retained in return for a reduction or abolition of the tariff on British goods. The Wellington government grew worried as the farmers asked this question with increasing earnestness, and at last sent a cable in October, 1933, to London.

It read as follows: "There is a widespread belief on the part of producers in New Zealand that if we undertook a drastic reduction or removal of New Zealand's protective tariff on United Kingdom goods His Majesty's Government in the United Kingdom would guarantee continuance of unrestricted entry of New Zealand's primary products." Would the British government kindly indicate its attitude toward this suggestion? The British government took two months to frame a negative answer. The suggestion would involve modification of the policy of planned marketing; it was "put forward by particular trade interests," and "could hardly be considered with reference to New Zealand alone." A cheerless answer.

Two months later another cable reached London asking more questions. The dairy farmers wished to know where they stood and what Britain might be planning. The answer gave them little satisfaction, for it implied that regulation was inevitable but that the amount of it could not be foreseen. All through the reply ran the thesis that only by limiting the amount of produce put on the market could prices be brought to a profitable level for all who supplied it. It was better for dominion and foreign producers to make a profit on the smaller quantity of goods they were allowed to send than to heap the market high with goods and thus drive prices to a ruinous depth.

What might have happened if the first reply had been in the affirmative we need not stop to consider. Had the question been asked prior to 1932 the answer would certainly have been "Yes," and those who dreamed of Empire free trade would have thought their dreams were about to come true. But the question would not have been asked then, for no one in the dominions (or in England) imagined that the British door would ever swing against their primary produce.

Among Australians, Mr. Bruce, former prime minister and now high commissioner in London, admits that it was necessary for the British government to help agriculture. He has urged his own government and the others to take steps of their own accord to restrict exports and set up marketing machinery to deal with quotas and control exports. Meanwhile he suggests that Britain should decide how far she wishes to go in her agricultural policy, remembering the extent to which the dominions depend on her for their markets. Britain is "the only market in the world of real interest to the agricultural countries. . . . We are all dependent on a prosperous Britain as a market for the things we want to sell." In return the dominions should reconsider, with the welfare of their primary exports in mind, the return they can offer. "The dominions will have to have the rule put over them as to what they can give to Britain in return for what she can give." [8]

This suggestion virtually means that Britain should cry halt to her policy of agricultural expansion and that the dominions should do likewise with their plans for industrial development. Each must recognize that first things must be put first, and that secondary considerations be kept second. There will still be plenty of room for industries in the dominions, and a big home market for the British farmer; but there should be less stress on artificial stimulation.

This view may possibly prevail, and the dominions may find it expedient to offer lower tariffs and/or increased preference in return for, or in anticipation of, better entry into the British market. While farm exports were safe, industrial protection could be developed without fear of consequences or weighing of price. At the next imperial conference the dominions will be obliged to offer a higher price for the concessions they seek. They will doubtless strive to secure a larger place in the British market at the expense of foreign producers, and will urge among other reasons the fact that they can take British emigrants while Denmark and the Argentine can not.

Another result is, however, possible. The dominions may seek more earnestly for other markets. In submitting the New Zealand tariff revision of 1934 the minister said New Zealand "should make a strong effort to negotiate with other countries, especially highly industrialized countries, which offer possibilities for the disposal of our

[8] *Times Weekly Edition*, August 2, 1934.

primary products." The list of possible countries is a very short one and alternative buyers of mutton, wool, and butter are not easily found.

Australia is thinking along the same line, and has recently become conscious of the importance of the Orient as a customer for her wool and wheat. Japan ranks second to Great Britain as a buyer of her wool, and takes a quarter of the clip, in addition to large quantities of wheat, tallow, and metals. Of the goods she sends in return, half do not compete with Australian wares, but two-thirds do compete with British imports. She buys from Australia three times as much as she sells to her; she would like to sell more, but the preferential tariff helps to prevent her from doing so.

Faced with possible restriction and reduction of her food exports to Britain, and given a hint that Japan might seek supplies from those who are better customers, Australia has become more favorably or anxiously disposed toward her northern neighbor and toward such other customers as Germany, France, Belgium, and Italy. Her prime minister has announced his intention to seek amendment of the Ottawa agreement in which Australia promised Britain a certain minimum preference and bound herself to be guided by the Tariff Board. When in 1934 the Italian government decided to cut imports of Australian wool in half in an effort to balance its trade with Australia, and when Germany shut out wool imports because it had no available foreign credits with which to pay for them, Australia was forcibly reminded that not all her trade was imperial, and began negotiations with London seeking to secure such a waiving of

British Ottawa rights as would permit her to make a new trade agreement with Italy. Yet almost on the same day she raised the duty on certain cotton cloths. For the possible benefit of a handful of cotton-growers and textile workers she risked giving annoyance to her British and Japanese customers, and shopkeepers in Lancashire began to cry for a boycott of Australian produce.

The path of the imperial economist in depression days is thus a stony road. Bargaining is difficult when sentiment is mixed with huckstering. It is hard between adults and adolescents, between countries which have established interests and countries which wish to establish interests. It becomes complicated when one cabinet minister is seeking to foster one interest while a second is devoting his attention to another. If the President of the Board of Trade tries to push the exchange of British manufactures for Argentine beef, it is embarrassing to find that the Minister of Agriculture is trying to check the purchase of that beef for the benefit of British stock-raisers; but his annoyance is small compared with that felt by the Secretary for the Dominions.

The situation is not new. Professor Nettels, in discussing the old colonial system of the eighteenth century, says, "The British political method of 1763 was to grant a favor here and a favor there as need arose. . . . Each issue that arose was treated on its merits, under the pressure of special groups and interests. . . . And because such favors were granted to different groups whose interests conflicted, the resulting policy was inevitably contradictory in some respects. The assumption behind all acts was that the colonies were valuable as sources of supply and as markets: the contradictions arose because conflicting interests were seeking profit through the application of general principles in which nearly everybody believed." [9] Failure to reconcile contradictions helped to end the First British Empire. Failure to reconcile the far greater contradictions between home and dominion interests may injure the Third.

[9] Curtis Nettels, "The Place of Markets in the Old Colonial System," *New England Quarterly*, 6:512 (1933).

CHAPTER SIX

BATTLES, BARGAINS, BOATS, AND BUILDINGS

WHEN THE NEW COMMERCIAL POLICY WAS PRESENTED TO parliament early in 1932 seven virtues were claimed for it. It would "transfer to our own factories and our own fields work which is now done elsewhere"; in preceding chapters we have seen the extent to which this has been done. But at the same time it would be used to maintain and expand exports. There would be increased imperial preferences, there would be reciprocal treaties, and there would be threats of retaliation against countries which discriminated against British wares. The story of the preferences has been told. That of the other two measures can be briefly set forth; in the light of American hopes for expanding exports it has a special interest.

For fifty years British protectionists had contended that a free trade country was helpless in face of attack. Other governments, and even dominions, raised their tariff walls with impunity, and there could be no effective action to make them stay their hand. Mr. Baldwin in 1932 rapped the knuckles of those who declared that the new commercial policy would lead to trade wars. Had not Britain been in such a war for decades? War was war, even if one side was shelled without being able to answer. The government was asking for a spade with which to dig deeper the trade channels to countries that were willing to reciprocate, and for a sword with which to strike back at countries that put discriminatory obstacles in the way of British wares.

Two years have sufficed to show the possibilities and difficulties of bilateral reciprocity and retaliation in a period when trade policy functions through quotas and exchange control, rather than through simple tariff levies, and when all manner of additional surtaxes, primage duties, and so forth may be piled on top of the original duty.

Retaliation fought its first campaign in a tariff war with France. In 1933 the French government decided to reduce import quotas by three-fourths on goods from countries not prepared to bargain for their retention at the old figures. From the negotiations that followed between France and various other countries Britain drew the deduction that she was being subjected to discrimination. Discussion between Paris and London failed to remove the grievance, and finally the President of the Board of Trade told the French that he would "very reluctantly have to take immediate retaliatory action by imposing additional duties on a range of French products unless within ten days the quotas are restored." France declined to budge, and Britain piled additional duties of 20 per cent on some important French goods. France replied by denouncing an old navigation treaty of 1826, which regulated shipping between the two countries, as well as a commercial convention of 1882, which contained provision for most-favored-nation treatment and forbade either country to discriminate against the other.

The war was on, and a British minister said, "If it is

to be a question of a trial of strength between the two countries, then the quicker we get down to facts the better." France cut the coal quota further. Negotiations were opened, but closed in failure; the quotas were further cut, and trade between the two countries fell steeply. Finally, in June, 1934, the conflict ended. The quota reductions and retaliatory duties were withdrawn, most-favored-nation terms were restored, tariff or quota adjustments were made, and Lyons, Manchester, Newcastle, and the French peasant could now try to repair the damage done to their trade. The episode was sharp, short, and instructive; it proved that Britain had a new weapon, that an armed man is prone to talk in belligerent terms, and that in war both sides suffer.

Meanwhile the strong right arm was being used against another old friend. Japan's remarkable expansion as exporter of cotton cloths was such that in 1933, for the first time, she sent abroad a slightly greater mileage of cottons than did Lancashire; in the first half of 1934 she beat Lancashire by more than a quarter. The depreciation of her currency to two-fifths of its gold value gave her a great advantage over sterling, for British currency had sunk only about half as much. Her cheap labor, good machinery, and large-scale organization added to her advantage, and the boycott of her goods in China turned her attention to other markets.

One of her greatest inroads was in India. Its effect was felt acutely both by the Indian cotton manufacturers, who supplied three-fourths of the native demand, and by Lancashire, which in 1929 had provided about two-thirds of the imports. By 1932 Japan had half the import trade.

In 1932 and 1933 the Indian government raised the duty on foreign cloths to 75 per cent, against a 25 per cent duty on British pieces. The Japanese manufacturers retorted with a threat to boycott Indian raw cotton, which was one of their chief raw materials, but representatives of the Indian and Japanese governments got together at Simla, and after long discussion reached agreement.

Japan was allowed to send a certain quantity of cottons to India unconditionally at a reduced duty; beyond that quantity the amount she could sell was proportionate to the amount of raw cotton she bought, and the total quantity was limited to a figure far below her sales during 1932. The market she lost was to be fought for between Lancashire and Indian manufacturers, and another big branch of world trade was subjected to the statistician and the turnstile.

At Simla agreement was reached; in London there was no such happy ending. There Japanese industrialists, at the invitation of the British government, met Lancashire rivals. Though the discussions were between economic groups, each had behind it, or over it, the power of its government. The very nature of the negotiators made failure inevitable. A sick industry was trying to persuade a healthy, expanding, and confident rival to surrender its advantages, to give much in return for little, to accept limits to its activities. Further, Lancashire asked that the whole world trade, and not merely the market controlled by Britain, be rationed out. To this the Japanese replied that they could not restrict their exports "without any obligation on Great Britain," and that while they were willing to consider "quantitative agreement" in the markets that were "within the influence of Great Brit-ain, . . . restriction applying to all markets of the world" was impracticable. They claimed, moreover, that to suggest the elimination of "cutthroat competition" was illiberal and uneconomic, since it was not cutting their throats; they deserved what they had gained because they alone among the nations of the world had organized themselves for efficiency in production and cheapness of product.

According to the economic theory the western world had taught them, they were right. They were talking to an industry which had done little to shake itself out of old habits and organization, an industry of which the friendly *Manchester Guardian* said that "reorganization for efficiency is a task still to be faced," [1] and of which the *Times* said the leaders would "do well to concentrate on the urgent task of reorganization which has been out-standing for so many years." [2] They were guests in a country where many had rejoiced over the aid given by a depreciated currency in undercutting rivals and gain-ing markets. Finally, while their cheap cottons and ray-ons had partly taken existing markets from rivals, they had also created and served a new market among the poor of Asia and Africa, a market that could not be sup-plied by the dearer goods of Europe. [3]

When discussions failed and diplomacy did no better, the British government proceeded to impose a quota on foreign textile imports into such parts of the colonial

[1] *Manchester Guardian Weekly*, March 16, 1934.
[2] *Times Weekly Edition*, March 22, 1934.
[3] See K. K. Kawakami, "Britain's Trade War with Japan," *Foreign Affairs*, April, 1934.

empire as it controlled. London could not tell the dominions what to do, for they managed their own trade policies. In some colonial areas "open door" treaties forbade restrictive action, but in others London could dictate or urge strongly. The quota was based on the cotton and rayon imports from each country into each colony between 1927 and 1931, a period when Japanese exports were much smaller than they had become later. It may deprive Japan of a market for a hundred million yards; this is about 5 per cent of her total exports, an amount that will hardly cripple her or bring the bloom of health back to Lancashire's cheeks.

London's action was a serious step on more than economic grounds, for it might have repercussions on imperial relations. The quota was a step toward closing the doors of the colonial market against foreign trade, an installment of economic imperialism in the crown colonies. Some of those colonies must grin and bear the loss of cheap goods and of the customs duties once collected from them. But those which had some degree of self-government might protest, while the self-governing dominions would pursue their own courses at angles that might be different from that of Great Britain.

Some of these things have already happened. In Ceylon, which is part way between a dependency and a dominion, the board of ministers — the cabinet — refused to introduce into the legislature a bill imposing the quota suggested by London. The reason was apparently that such action would deprive the poor of the only textiles they could afford. Faced with this refusal, the British government imposed the quota on Ceylon by an Order in Council. It had power to do so, since the new constitution of 1931 "reserved" for the crown certain rights of veto or of action. The effect of the quota on Ceylon's imports will be serious; the effect of the Order on imperial relations may be still more serious.

In the dominions the British action struck no responsive chord. Australia and Canada export far more goods to Japan than they draw from that source, and the competition of cheap Japanese goods with their own products is slight. Australians have noted the fact that Japan's woolen industry is expanding in a manner resembling the growth of the cotton industry. This causes an increased demand for wool, and an antagonized Japan might seek elsewhere for its raw material. In the circuitous language of a letter issued in 1934 by the Bank of New South Wales, "the trend in Great Britain towards a diminution in imports of foodstuffs raises still further difficulties, and in face of the rapid growth of Japanese industry it is difficult to resist the conclusion that any survey of the rational ends of Australian trade policy in the circumstances of today must offer a more prominent place to interchange of goods in the East than it has occupied in the past." [4] If therefore Britain tries to use political means to cramp Japanese exports Australia must act by herself.

Britain's commercial new dealers were ready to fight, but hoped to be able to reciprocate. Like President Roosevelt, they wished, through trade agreements, to give privileges to such countries as were willing to confer favors in return, even though their hands were tied

[4] Printed in the *Manchester Guardian Weekly*, May 18, 1934.

in part by the Ottawa pacts and then by the development of the agricultural policy.

The first question to be answered was "With what countries can agreements be made?" The answer was almost as hard to find in London as in Washington, but just as Cuba seemed a natural starting point for American pacts, Scandinavia, the young Baltic republics, and the Argentine were the most natural areas for a British approach. They were tied to sterling. They depended chiefly on the British market for the sale of their farm and forest products; combined, they were good customers for British goods, and some of their buying might be transferred from Germany or Poland to Britain. They had no powerful desire to become self-sufficing industrially, as had the dominions. They had no coal, their industries were small and specialized, and they imported many manufactured articles.

In all, thirteen trade agreements had been made up to August, 1934, with all three Scandinavian countries, with Finland, Latvia, Argentina, and other primary producing countries. In them lower tariffs, a guaranteed minimum share of British purchases from foreign countries, or a minimum quantity of purchases of certain commodities are given by Great Britain. The treaty may offer entry, free of duty or of quantitative control, to farm products, subject however to the proviso that restriction may be imposed later, under fixed quota or quantity limitations, as part of a marketing scheme. In return, Britain gets tariff reductions, and an assured quantity or proportion of the purchases, especially of certain commodities. Latvia agrees to buy a certain quantity of British herrings each year, and to purchase 70 per cent of her coal from British mines. In Denmark the coal quota is 80 per cent, in Norway 70 per cent, in Sweden 47 per cent. There is also an agreement, containing coal clauses, with Germany.

Some of these agreements have now been in operation for over a year, and first results can be examined. The trade statistics for the first half of 1934 show that British trade with Scandinavia and the Baltic is almost back to the level of 1929. For this the trade agreements can claim some credit, but membership in the sterling group and the building boom have also helped. Norway and Denmark have done better than they promised as coal buyers, but Sweden has fallen a little short of her word. In the three Scandinavian countries and Germany purchases of British coal have risen to 2,500,000 tons in one year, and while some of this is due to recovery some of it represents the displacement of Polish and German coal. But those gains have been offset by losses elsewhere, for competition has been intensified in other markets, especially in Italy, where Poland and Germany got in ahead of Britain and showed that they too could make barter bargains. Poland agreed to exchange Italian ships for Polish coal, Germany took Italian foodstuffs and gave coal for them. Hence while some English mines have benefited from increased trade with the Baltic, South Wales mines have lost trade in the Mediterranean.

Of the Scandinavian countries Denmark was most closely tied to the British market. If she lost her grip on the British breakfast table, where else could she turn to sell her butter and bacon? She sold far more to Britain than she bought there, and knew that in political discussions, where invisible exports and triangular or polygonal trade are too abstruse for consideration, her case would seem bad. She therefore tried to strengthen her claim for generous treatment. She had a "Buy British" campaign and organized a British Industrial Exhibition in Copenhagen. Her Exchange Control Board steered buyers toward British goods rather than those of other countries. Importers could buy plenty of pounds, but few dollars; it was easy to buy and pay for British goods, but hard to secure credits with which to buy American or other wares. Her position is precarious, however, for her staple exports are goods which are or soon will be subject to marketing schemes and quotas. She is guaranteed 62 per cent of the British purchases of foreign bacon, but if those purchases are reduced, as they have been more than once, her shipments will fall further. Already Danish voices are raised pointing out that British sales must fall if British purchases are reduced, just as in the Argentine leaders have asserted that the country must seek markets and goods elsewhere if beef imports are further curtailed. Again we come back to the difficulties created by the emergence of the British farmer and by the use of quotas as the way to his salvation.

The search for markets by trade pacts found one of its most curious results in Russia. The Labor government in 1930 made an agreement with Russia; its successor decided to end it, largely because of the pressure brought to bear at Ottawa. This decision did not end trade between the two countries, and the building boom of 1933 brought vast quantities of Russian lumber across the North Sea. But Russia bought far less than she sold; in 1933 the ratio was 1 to 4. Here then was a good potential customer.

In February, 1934, a bargain was struck, in one of the queerest trade agreements extant. In the first place, it tried to fit in the Ottawa decree against dumping. The usual most-favored-nation clause was qualified by the provision that if British preference to dominion products was frustrated or if home production was injured by excessive Russian offerings at low prices, Britain could point out this fact. If negotiations failed to end the frustration, the entry of the offending goods could be limited or prohibited.

In the second place the balance was to be redressed. Soviet payments (for goods, services, etc.) were to bear annually an increasing ratio to Soviet proceeds on sales to Britain. The ratio of payments to proceeds in 1934 was to be 1 to 1.7, and was to draw year by year toward a ratio of 1 to 1.1 in 1938. In calculating it, British invisible exports in the form of shipping earnings, etc., were to be included as a fixed percentage of the trade turnover, and the Soviet promised to use more British ships in so far as they were available at prevailing market rates. This promise is being well kept, and the purchase of British goods has increased considerably.

This is a curiously hedged and conditional bargain. Russia must not frustrate in her selling and she must buy with an eye on a ratio. What will happen if she fails to come up to the mark is not clear. The important fact is that an agreement has been made with a British government which has among its followers the most violent anti-Bolshevik elements of the British population. Thus we pass one step further away from the phobias of the war years.

The new commercial policy was, by judicious use of protection, "to enable and encourage our people to render their methods of production and distribution more efficient." One would expect producers to be sufficently alive to their own interests and eager to make their methods more efficient without state encouragement; but the experience of almost every country disproves this, and depression governments have played the rôle of Good Samaritan, caring for the sick rather than aiding the strong.

The iron and steel industry was the first patient. The Imports Advisory Committee recommended that it be protected with a 33⅓ per cent duty till October, 1934, provided it undertook a thorough reorganization. Protection was not to be regarded as a cloak for incompetence and would be withdrawn if competence was not sought and found. The Committee appointed a group of iron and steel men to prepare a scheme; they worked out a plan for a central organization with far-reaching powers, and with teeth and claws to be used on firms which clung to old ways. There was to be amalgamation and grouping; production and sale were to be regulated. But when the plan was submitted to the whole industry the far-reaching parts were cut out, the teeth and claws removed, the powers of the central body curtailed, and the objectives watered down to vague phrases about providing for the "maximum manufacturing and commercial efficiency throughout the industry" and the expansion of the export trade.

This plan was accepted by most of the units of the industry, and was regarded by the Imports Advisory Committee as satisfactory. The Committee therefore recommended that the time limit in the tariff be removed. The industry thus gets permanent protection. How far it will carry out its part of the bargain and use the machinery it has set up remains to be seen. The import duty is high enough to permit exploitation of metal users by producers, and reorganization may mean price maintenance rather than improved production methods and lower costs to consumers.

Experience in this industry, as in coal and cotton, has shown the difficulties that stand in the way of reorganization. Small minorities may obstruct, delay inordinately, and impair seriously plans that would benefit the industry as a whole. Those minorities may consist of small producers who fear they will be crushed: in America we have seen the hostility that can be aroused when "the little fellow" is endangered. Or they may be big, efficient, and successful units that resent having their freedom of action curtailed for the protection of weaker rivals. Hence while onlookers and many who are engaged in industry agree that "the simple patterns of a laissez faire economy" which the nineteenth century developed do not function well in the world of today, reform is very difficult.

The difficulties are well seen in the Lancashire cotton industry. The many plans for its remodeling include price regulation in order to stop fierce undercutting of prices, combination of independent firms both horizontally and vertically, the scrapping of obsolete or redundant plant, and better marketing organization. But the spinning trade "has never yet been able to secure the support of one hundred per cent of the spindles concerned for any of its schemes," even the most modest and gentle.[5]

The feeling is growing more widespread that under such conditions government aid must be enlisted, in order to compel recalcitrant minorities to accept plans and rules that the majority voluntarily accept. State intervention has already achieved some necessary results which industry itself would probably never have reached: the merging of the railroads into four systems and the nation-wide electrical scheme are the chief instances. In the United States similar problems of the railroads, the soft coal fields, and the oil fields seem to be incapable of solution without government action. If intervention goes further, it will be largely the fault of industry itself; it would not surprise us as it might have done two decades ago; and it would fit in with a truism of economic history that periods of free individual enterprise have been few, far apart, and brief.

Of all sick British industries the last to call on the doctor was shipping. It was almost the most important caller, for shipping services are the country's largest export commodity, larger than cottons or coal. But ship-

[5] *Manchester Guardian Weekly*, December 23, 1933. The *Economist*, July 21, 1934, says the industry has languished for more than a decade for lack of coherent leadership; "the time is surely coming when public opinion will cease to tolerate the impotence of mismanagement in the sacred name of individualism."

ping is more than an occupation: it is a national subject, part of the country's life and being. Mr. Runciman, President of the Board of Trade and a shipowner, voiced an article in the national creed when he said in December, 1933, "To us, an island people who are dependent on sea communication, an adequate mercantile marine is the first necessity of our existence. We have no intention of allowing its existence to be imperiled." Kipling put the matter more picturesquely when he wrote

> The bread that you eat and the biscuits you nibble,
> The sweets that you suck and the joints that you carve,
> They are brought to you daily by all us big steamers,
> And if anyone hinders our coming — you'll starve.

The Germans knew that bit of Kipling and nearly proved its truth with their submarines.

Today it is the "big steamers" and not "you" that starve. In British ports and backwaters over four hundred vessels, with a net tonnage of over a million tons, lie idle. Last year there were twice as many, and in a shipyard on the Clyde the partly finished hull of a giant 73,000-ton greyhound stood deserted of workmen because there was no money with which to complete the job. The cause of this shipping tragedy was that while the available shipping supply grew by more than half between 1913 and 1933 the amount of cargo asking to be carried grew slowly and then collapsed one-third after 1929. British ships still carried about two-fifths of it, but competition between British boats and between them and those carrying foreign flags was intense. Shipping freights were among the first charges to fall back to pre-war levels and then sink below.

In the rivalry of flags, subsidies given by some governments for building and operating ships queered the pitch, for the bounty-fed boats could quote rates or attain a speed which unsubsidized vessels could not meet. The size of all shipping subsidies has been estimated at $150,000,000 a year. The importance of these grants has probably been exaggerated, for the British tramp steamer, that general utility cargo vessel which will go anywhere and carry almost anything, found its hottest competitors among the unsubsidized vessels of Scandinavia or among boats carrying the same flag as itself. With a swollen shipping supply and a shrinking volume of cargo, depression was inevitable, and a protectionist policy in Britain made it more so; but the subsidies have accentuated the competition on some trade routes, especially to South Africa and India.

By the end of 1933 the situation had become so bad that shipowners began to call for aid. They asked for almost every form of subsidy, retaliation, discrimination, and reciprocity that has ever been devised. Their proposals led far, but not in the right direction. Discrimination against foreign flags might be a boomerang on a country that still carried two-fifths of the world's ocean cargoes. It would prove a pretext for costly retorts. A straight subsidy cured nothing, was hard to administer, and might justify a claim for similar aid from cotton and coal. Eventually, in July, 1934, the government made certain conditional offers to the shipowners. They could borrow money very cheaply in order to build new boats or modernize old ones: but they must scrap three tons of old ships for every new ton. This plan would get rid of surplus tonnage and give work to shipbuilding; but the shipowners rejected the offer.

The second offer was a little more to their taste. The government would provide tramp steamers with a subsidy of £2,000,000 for a year, provided the owners would formulate a scheme that would prevent British tramps from squandering the money in competition with each other and would insure more work for British vessels at the expense of foreign subsidized boats. Further, the tramp owners must strive through their international organizations to get a general adjustment of tonnage to demand, while the government would do its part by discussing with other powers steps toward the abolition of subsidies and the reduction of tonnage. It would also confer with the dominions to see if imperial trade could be put on a basis that "is more restricted than is the rule at present" — a remark that suggests an attempt to revive features of the seventeenth century navigation laws.

The whole plan is so liberally dotted with conditions and hopes for unlikely foreign and dominion collaboration that no great result can be expected. The subsidy may become part of the varied public alms, and its smallness is a defect that can be rectified.

While the homely tramps were offered their modest subsidy, the unfinished Cunard greyhound on the Clyde won practical sympathy. Lack of funds had caused the suspension of work on a boat which was to be the biggest and fastest in the world, and which would bring back the blue ribbon of the North Atlantic snatched from British hands by a German ship and then taken by an Italian. In December, 1933, the Cunard and White

Star lines agreed to merge in one company, and the government offered to advance £3,000,000 for the completion of the ship and half that amount as working capital for the new company. It also hinted its willingness to lend money for the building of a sister ship.

Two great fleets were thus united, with twenty-five famous boats, and to the sound of bagpipes workers once more trooped into the Clydeside shipyard. But the launching of the giant vessel in September, and the races which in the fullness of time it will run with its French, German, and Italian rivals, will have little more effect on the fortunes of British shipping than the birth of a Derby winner has on British animal husbandry. The world's shipping consists not of super-liners, but of thousands of middle-sized and small cargo boats; and their life depends on international trade, a trade that can only revive as prosperity returns and as the wave of economic nationalism spends its force.

The provision of money for the giant Cunarder was one of the few attempts made to stimulate production by an outlay of public funds. The belief that prosperity could be restored or depression greatly mitigated if the government "made work" had grown weaker in the light of experience. To make a deep impression on unemployment figures, colossal schemes would be necessary, at an expenditure that could not be faced until interest rates had fallen from their high post-war level. But at the back of the Englishman's mind was a conviction that one big job must be attempted whenever the time was favorable. That job was the attack on the slum.

Ever since the war the housing problem has been

acute, for two reasons. In the first place, building was suspended during the war, and the arrears had to be made good. In the second place, public opinion became increasingly disturbed concerning the quality of the housing conditions in parts of its large cities. There were in 1933 about three hundred thousand houses unfit for human habitation, and seven hundred thousand almost as bad. In these million houses five million people lived — about one-eighth of the total population. There was thus a double task — the erection of more houses and of better houses. When Mr. Lloyd George in an election speech made just after the armistice promised to build homes fit for heroes to dwell in he gave a pledge, the fulfillment of which was as urgent as it was difficult.

The difficulty was largely one of cost. Materials and land were costly, wages were high, and interest rates were heavy. When the house was built the local taxes on it were large. Yet in spite of high costs, the wage-earning classes must have dwellings that could be rented at between $1.50 and $3 a week "clear," leaving the land-lord to pay the taxes out of that amount. Given these conditions, the building of houses for tenants did not pay. The net return on capital was far less than could be obtained in other directions. The nineteenth century assumption that private enterprise would always provide houses broke down, and the much-condemned speculative jerry-builder of Victorian days had now to be thought of with a little more kindness. At least he did put a roof of a sort over England's head, and did it cheaply. His descendants could not do that, so the state must step in where they stepped out.

Since 1918 governments of all colors have given financial aid. The Conservatives gave subsidies to private builders, Labor gave subsidies to local authorities who would undertake building operations. Between them they contributed to the erection of nearly 1,200,000 homes. Meanwhile more than a million houses have been built without public assistance, but largely with the aid of a thousand building societies. Yet neither public nor private action could break the barrier between the poorer wage-earners and good cheap houses. The better-paid artisans and the middle class were the chief beneficiaries, for even the subsidized houses often had to be let at rents beyond the reach of the lower wage levels. The million hovels remained to challenge the nation's conscience.

In 1933 the supply of cheap long-term credit made private building possible on a larger scale, and in 1933–1934 over two hundred thousand houses were built without state aid. Public enterprise built nearly a hundred thousand, and more than half of the total new supply was for lower-paid workers. In addition, an attack could now be made on the slums, and in 1933 a five-year plan for slum clearance was formulated. Local authorities were invited to prepare and submit schemes to the Ministry of Health. By March, 1934, virtually all of them had done so, most of their plans had been approved, and some of them had been completed.

These plans provide for the demolition of almost all the three hundred thousand dwellings that come under the legal definition of a slum, i. e., a dwelling not fit for human habitation and incapable of being made so at a reasonable cost. The near-slums will be dealt with later, by reconditioning or by demolition. The first job will rehouse 1,200,000 persons; the cost will be about £125,000,000, and will be met partly by state subsidy and partly from local taxes. The rents are expected to be no higher than those formerly paid for a slum dwelling. About a hundred thousand workers will be directly and indirectly employed, but the effect will not be limited to them, and the project will remove the worst blot from the urban map. If it is followed up by an attack on the near-slums, it will bring one of the most unpleasant problems of modern social life and health within sight of solution and be one compensation for the depression.

Our concern in the preceding pages has been chiefly with public policy, and it must now be very apparent that the British state has been as active as has the American. The emphasis has differed, for the depression struck at different points. There was little need to protect further the American market, for competitive imports were negligible. There was no need to buttress the British banking and financial system, for its reserve of strength was even greater than had been imagined. Britain has relied less on public expenditure and initiative, and more on making the road open again for the resumption of private initiative; even her marketing schemes and plans for industrial reorganization show a greater willingness to leave the actual formulation and operation of control in the hands of producers themselves. She has thrown her weight behind regimentation, but it has been in a large measure self-regimentation.

Of her many policies it would be fruitless guesswork to predict possible effects. The home market has revived and the local producer's grasp on it has been strengthened. But little has been done, except in limited fields, in recovering overseas markets. The home demand may soon reach the limit of its capacity to buy, and saturation point may come. If recovery means a regaining of the condition of material welfare enjoyed in 1929, or still more in 1913, there must be a large expansion of overseas trade. For that expansion the country has lost the competitive advantage of superior resources and of an earlier start that it held in the old industries, and has no such advantage in the production of the newer commodities that the world wants today.

Professor G. C. Allen in his *British Industries and Their Organisation* (1933) finds it impossible to state with confidence that in the future Britain's advantages as an industrial center will be sufficient to enable her to maintain a dense population at the old standard of living; and the sky has shown few signs of the restoration of those conditions of easy international interchange in which she can make an effort to do so. If trade treaties are essential to the restoration of those conditions, it will be time to rejoice when pacts have been made with the United States, France, Japan, Italy, and other old large customers, and when peace has come to the Irish Sea. If those conditions do not return, if international trade is to diminish in importance before the spread of economic self-sufficiency and the dispersion of industrial plants over the world, and if the advantages once enjoyed are gone forever, Great Britain may join the list of nations whose customers found new servants or learned how to serve themselves.

Man, fortunately, does not live or recover by politics alone, and when the historian is able to look back on these years he will probably attach little importance to some of the policies we have examined. He may dismiss many of them as mad, futile things done in a mad world that was playing tit for tat. He may quote with approval Mr. Clay's confession of hope:

"I look for recovery rather to the diffused initiative of the more intelligent and enterprising traders, financiers, and engineers engaged in industry in this and other countries. I look to them to find openings for the employment of the unemployed, by discovering new wants that are unsatisfied and means of satisfying them at a price the consumer can pay, new processes that will make it possible to stimulate a resumption of trade by price cuts that involve no loss, and new commercial connections to replace markets that have been lost or spoiled. And the greatest aid that governments could give to trade recovery would be to remove the impediments and handicaps that hamper the exercise of this initiative." [6]

It may be that work which industrial scientists and engineers are doing today will bring new industries into being or give new strength to sick ones, as more economical ships are designed, as coal becomes a greater source of liquid fuel, and as other new productive and consuming possibilities are unfolded. Recovery in the past has nearly always been stimulated by some new commodity, some new technique, or the development of a new era. It may be so in the future.

[6] In *The World's Economic Crisis and the Way of Escape* (1932), p. 153.

On the other hand our imaginary historian may have to record that the political obsession with economic defense and self-sufficiency took nations back further and further into their shells, to the great discomfort of those whose shells were too small to hold them. He may find that the chief result of depression superimposed on war was such a drawing apart of the nations and such a festering of sores that western capitalism, and the civilization of which it is such a large part, earned the verdict suggested by Mr. Fay — "Suicide whilst of unsound mind."

CHAPTER SEVEN

AUSTRALIA
"FIRST IN AND FIRST OUT"

To MOST NORTH AMERICANS AUSTRALIA IS A BIG DISTANT island, with a lot of sheep, some strange animals and stranger vowels. It once invented and exported the Australian ballot, and since then has been an incorrigible experimenter in social legislation or state enterprise. That a country with such a reputation should seek new and unorthodox ways of meeting a crisis is only natural, and when Australians claim that they were "first into the depression and first out of it" we may with profit examine the secrets behind the second of these pioneering achievements.

The setting for the story can be briefly described. Productive Australia consists of six and a half million people, who dwell on the more or less fertile south, east, and southwestern fringes of the continent. Two-thirds of them live in towns, mining, making the goods or rendering the services that can only be done on the spot, or working in the factories that have grown up behind the political protection of a high tariff and the geographical protection of long distance from outside sources of supply.

If productive Australia is town and country, exporting Australia is all country, sending out primary products to feed people and machines. Of these products wool towers above all others, and wheat comes next. From 1923 to 1928 wool accounted for nearly half the total exports, wheat for about a fifth, and if we add meat, hides, flour, and tallow we find that the pastoralist and the grain-grower supplied three-fourths of the continent's export commodities.

The pastoralist, who is Australia's frontiersman, has been buffeted by man and by nature. Hostile land and tax laws hit him if he seemed too big; rising tariffs and wages added to his costs of production and consumption. He was fair game in every plan for extending settlement and cultivation, and was gradually pushed back into the arid lands in order to make room for the plough, the dairy cow, and the fruit tree. Devastating droughts decimated his flocks. But he stuck to his job, improved his breeds, conserved such water as he could get, and when the edge of adversity had been dulled began again to build up his flocks. Canada might lead the world as wheat exporter, the United States could be hog and cotton king, but in wool production the Austrian pastoralist was supreme. The world went to him for two-fifths of its woolen fibers, and Australia learned in 1929 how much the welfare of her cities depended on him.

Australian exports in 1928 were worth approximately £140,000,000. They absorbed a third of the country's total production and probably supplied nearly a quarter of its national income. Prosperity among the exporters reacted on everybody, and during the twenties it was great. High prices prevailed, the wool clip rose by half in five years, and the wheat crop climbed a fifth. Since "export production plays a predominant part in determining the amount and nature of the national income," [1] the towns flourished when the countryside fared well.

The national income was fed by a second stream in the form of overseas borrowing. Like all new countries Australia needed capital for her development and had to draw much of it from outside. Private investment was large, but public borrowing was larger. Circumstances had decreed that the railroads be built and operated by the state, and a big land mass without navigable waterways needed much railroad equipment. In addition there was need for large outlays in roads, bridges, and harbors, in preparing land for closer settlement, in water conservation, and in making advances to settlers who were rich in willingness to work but poor in this world's goods.

In theory this loan capital was reproductive, for the equipment it provided would earn income or increase the productivity and the tax yield of the country. In practice this was not always so; many projects were unwise or too costly, and failed either to earn enough to pay the interest on the money spent or to add much to tax capacity. Such disappointments are not peculiar to Australia, but whereas the cost of mistakes or of overoptimism in equipping the United States with railroads was borne largely by private investors the cost in Australia remained a permanent dead-weight part of the national debt.

In the decade following the war borrowing for inter-

[1] D. B. Copland, *Australia in the World Crisis, 1929–1933* (1934), p. 12. This book is the most recent and authoritative account of Australian developments, and is written by the head of the Australian brain trust. See also E. R. Walker, *Australia in the World Depression,* (1933).

nal development went on at a rapid pace, for prospects were bright and two new lenders had been found. John Bull was as willing as ever to lend, Uncle Sam was now opening his pockets, and the war had shown that large loans could be raised inside the country. If America's rake's progress was in the stock market, Australia's was in the loan market. In five years the external debt rose £150,000,000, and the internal debt half as much. The expenditure of this money created a demand for goods and gave much employment on public works.

Australia's income was therefore fed by the proceeds of exports worth £140,000,000 a year on the eve of the depression, and by loans from abroad averaging £30,000,000 a year. These two sources contributed about a quarter of her total income. She had to meet an overseas interest bill of about £27,000,000, but the new loans comfortably paid that, and the money she received for her exports was consequently available to pay for her imports. But if anything happened to diminish or dry up these two streams, the country would suffer a severe drought.

That drought came in 1929 in full and double force, with the collapse of export prices and the cessation of overseas loans. This was in keeping with the experience of many other countries, for the fall in prices of primary products and the damming of the loan channels from London and New York were the first big indications that the new era had ended. At the Australian wool sales in 1929 wool that had sold for 45d. a pound in 1927 and for 41d. in 1928 fetched only 26d. "Greasy merino" dropped from 17d. to 11d. in one year and to 8d. in the next. Wheat prices fell a fifth in a year, and bad harvests reduced the yield by a quarter.

The effect of this on exports was a drop in one year from £140,000,000 to £100,000,000 and to £80,000,000 in two. In the meantime the stream of loans had dried up completely; the day of heavy lending and borrowing, with all that it had meant in additional income to the borrower, was ended. In consequence of these two losses, one-tenth of the total national income vanished in a year, and three-tenths in two years.

The broad features of the depression as it affected Australia were soon clear. The country had to pay its external interest bill and the cost of its imports out of the greatly shrunken credits obtained by the sale of its exports, and those credits were not big enough. Lack of loan funds stopped public works and spread unemployment among public workers and those who had supplied the goods they needed. Farmers and pastoralists saw their purchasing power cut down, and the cities felt the effect in rising unemployment among factory workers. Unemployment, which had been 9 per cent in 1929, rose relentlessly to 30 per cent in 1932, and in some industries to 40 per cent. Costs fell far less (or less quickly) than prices, and many enterprises became unprofitable. The stock market index number was cut in half. All this reacted on public finance, and deficits grew greater.

Like every other country, Australia met the early stages of disaster with expectation and expedients. She expected the storm to be as short as it was sharp, and so turned to the nearest and most obvious shelters within reach. Two immediate problems had to be faced. How could she meet her overseas bills on debts incurred or goods bought? How could she defray the costs of government at home?

The first question she answered by short-term borrowing in London, by drawing on the large credits which her banks fortunately had built up in London in better times, and by exporting gold from her domestic bank reserves. In one year she shipped nearly 60 per cent of those reserves overseas, and gave the Commonwealth Bank power to take over the gold of the other banks. She organized an exchange pool to mobilize the available supply of foreign exchange and insure that the government had the credits it needed to pay John and Sam. She took steps to reduce the amount due to outsiders by reducing the amount of goods bought from them. The tariff was raised, luxury imports were prohibited, and the entry of some goods was rationed.

An attempt was made to answer the second question by chipping off a little public spending here, adding a little taxation there, reducing loan expenditure, and borrowing from the banks. A director of the Bank of England was invited to visit the country in 1930, and when he gave the assembled premiers a lecture on "What's wrong with Australia?" his listeners promised to take drastic steps toward balancing their budgets by reducing their borrowing and curtailing their spending.

These measures were of little or limited value. The gold and London credits must be exhausted eventually. The higher tariff reduced customs receipts where it kept goods out, raised the cost of goods it let in, maintained the high prices of local products, and thus kept the cost of production of export goods too high; but it did help to reduce the volume of imports and ease the strain on exchange. Budgets were not, and could not be, balanced; ministers feared the political effect of reductions in the salaries and wages of public servants or of curtailment of public works, and reliance on bank loans to balance budgets was inevitable. Meanwhile export prices were sinking lower.

More drastic steps were necessary, and as 1930 ended the air grew thick with plans for all kinds of inflation or deflation. But time was gradually making the elements of the situation clearer, and events were soon to hasten a decision that would face the problem as a whole, and not merely look at that part of it which concerned the payment of external debts.

Three events led to decision and to a plan. The first was the abandonment by the banks in early 1931 of their attempt to peg the exchange rate near parity with sterling — which was still on gold. That attempt had been made partly perhaps from pride and dislike of a depreciated currency, and partly because it was evident that if the Australian pound sank to a discount of say 20 per cent, one hundred Australian pounds would pay only eighty pounds of interest in London. But the strain was too great; the demand for drafts on London was enormous, especially when talk of inflation drove people to get their money out of the country. Eventually therefore the banks pulled the peg out of the hole and drove it into one much lower. For nearly a year one had to give £130 Australian to buy £100 sterling, but in December, 1931, the price was reduced to £125, and there it still remains.

Australian currency was thus definitely depreciated in terms of sterling, and when sterling left gold and depreciated, the Australian pound was worth less than the sterling pound, which in turn was worth less than the gold pound.

What was the significance of this? Australia depreciated unwillingly, yet soon found that the price she paid brought her important compensations. As debtor she suffered, for she had to spend £125 or £130 to pay a debt of £100 in London; and when sterling was at its lowest point in terms of dollars her pound bought only about $2.80 in New York where once it had purchased $4.86. Yet she never defaulted on a loan. The importer paid the same high price for his goods, and this barrier, plus the higher tariff and various other charges, effectively reduced the volume of imports and cut their value down two-thirds. A depreciated exchange was probably a better method of restricting imports than was action at the customs office.

While governments and buyers of imports paid the price of depreciation, the benefit of depreciation came to the chief victim of the depression, the exporter, and took from his shoulders some of the load that was threatening to plunge him into insolvency. If he got £100 for his wheat or wool in London, that sum was worth £125 when it reached him. He got more Australian pounds for his produce than he would have received in sterling or gold, and it was in Australian pounds that he paid his debts and his production or consumption costs. His export price in sterling or gold would have averaged about 43 per cent of its 1928 level during the first half of 1931;

but in Australian pounds it was about 55 per cent. After England left gold, gold prices sank further, but sterling prices rose or remained steady, and he thus escaped the terrible price deflation which farmers in North America suffered. All through 1931 and 1932 his price index in Australian currency fluctuated between 50 and 60; had the country kept to parity with sterling it would have moved between 40 and 50, and if the country had stopped on gold it would have sunk during those years from 50 to 30.

This installment of salvation stimulated him to increased production. Good seasons helped, and he expanded his exports during those years to a volume beyond the pre-depression period. Thus he counterbalanced some of the fall in price, and did a little to keep up his income. The rest of the community paid some of the price in dearer imports and debt costs; the Australian, an inveterate traveler, could not afford to take trips to Europe, much less to America. But the country at large got something tangible in return in the saving of its primary producers.

The second important event of early 1931 was a decision by the Federal Arbitration Court to reduce *real* wages by 10 per cent. For thirty years Australia had been building state and federal machinery for the prevention of industrial disputes and of sweating. Wages boards and arbitration courts had been established, and in their deliberations the principle of a living wage had become accepted and elaborated. The principle had been translated into figures, and these figures were adjusted, either periodically or when appeals were made to the regulatory body, in accordance with movements in the official cost of living index number.

The living wage became the basis of Australian working conditions. It was regarded as almost sacrosanct, and any industry that could not afford to pay it had better close its doors or get an increase in the tariff. But in time of stress, during the depression of 1920–1922, the wages tribunals had taken "absence of prosperity" and the economic condition of suffering industries into account, and fixed wages below the accepted level. They had shown that the system was flexible enough to deal with depression and falling prices as well as with prosperity and rising prices.

When prices began to fall in 1929 the Federal Arbitration Court, the most important of all the tribunals, had reduced wages quarterly as the cost of living index fell. This reduced money costs to employers but left the purchasing power of wages untouched. In January, 1931, however, the Court departed from its usual simple calculation and automatic adjustment. It said that the loss of national income must be shared by wage-earners, and therefore reduced their wages one-tenth in buying power. In actual money, wages were now 20 per cent lower than in 1928, and as the cost of living sank further, they fell to 30 per cent; but their purchasing power was down only 10 per cent at most.

This reduction applied only to workers subject to Federal Court awards, and adjustments were made slowly by other wage-fixing authorities. There was delay, and some courts reduced nominal wages but not real ones; but even that caused an orderly reduction in the labor bill as prices fell. Thus for the second time the machinery proved itself capable of meeting changed circumstances and of subordinating sacrosanctity to economic realities. Australia had adjusted herself to post-war economic conditions with no serious labor disturbance, and again in 1931 quietly accepted the inevitable.

The third event was an ultimatum. In April, 1931, the Commonwealth Bank informed the Loan Council that it would loan no more money to governments. The Commonwealth Bank was set up in 1912 by a Labor government as an installment of socialistic finance; it had become controller of the note issue, was discharging increasingly the functions of a bankers' bank or central reserve bank, and was serving the government without becoming its tool. The Loan Council consisted of the treasurers of the federal and state governments. It was set up in 1924 to prevent undue competition and clashing in the raising of loans, and eventually became manager of the existing debt and controller of all future borrowing. Without its approval no new loans could be raised either inside or outside the country. Even before the depression it was applying the brake to borrowing, and when governments met deficits by borrowing from the Bank they had to work through the Loan Council. By 1931 they were in debt to the Bank for over £50,000,000, but, said the ultimatum, a point had been reached "beyond which it would be impossible . . . to provide further assistance for the governments in the future."

To that blunt announcement there could be only one reply — violent denunciation of the wickedness of the Bank and acceptance of its decision. The Loan Council appointed a committee which in turn appointed a sub-committee of treasury officials and four economists, to survey the field and recommend something. The suggestions made by this group were largely accepted and will go down in history as the Premiers' Plan.

That plan marked the end of makeshifts and half measures. It was the product of the hard thinking that Australian economists had been doing both before the storm broke and after. Twenty years ago a keen student of Australian affairs said:

"Australian democracy has never recognized a science which has formulated exact laws dealing with human wealth and welfare, and which limits the divine right of the democracy to achieve its will. It has never consulted professors of economics as to the possible result of its decrees, nor, when it has passed laws, has it carefully investigated and tabulated the results so as to guide future action. The democratic leaders have listened with impatience to the chorus of *non possumus* which came from the lips of the economists and have disregarded it." [2]

The correct retort to that boast is that in 1914 there were virtually no economists, either academic or otherwise, in Australia. The country had some splendid statisticians; but her Labor party had produced no great thinkers or writers, for its creed was "Socialism without doctrines," and the only three issues on which economic argument was ever serious — single tax, free trade, and bimetallism — were dead issues. In the universities, economics was regarded as a minor subject or as a dangerous

[2] F. W. Eggleston, "The Australian Democracy and Its Economic Problems," *Economic Journal*, September, 1915, p. 346.

one. In 1914 there was one professor of economics in one university; elsewhere one or two lectures were given weekly by men whose main work and interests lay in other fields. So far as Australia was concerned the "chorus of *non possumus*" was a solo.

This condition changed rapidly during the next decade, partly under the stimulus given to economic studies by the spread of university classes for wage- and salary-earners, and partly through a growing provision for commercial education. Teaching and research jumped ahead, and since no faculty was large enough to permit the division of labor that marks the large American universities, the Australian economist had to be a general practitioner. His contact with statisticians on one hand and with labor and business on the other made his work realistic and quantitative without its losing detachment, and like most Australian intellectuals he kept in touch with trends in the United States and Great Britain. He knew his Irving Fisher, Ely, and Taussig as well as his Marshall, Cannan, and Keynes, and his workingmen students had forced him to know his Henry George and Karl Marx. But he was far enough away from the temples of northern orthodoxy to permit an occasional excursion into heresy. Finally, the band to which he belonged was too small to permit division into many schools, and by correspondence and conference he and his fellows eventually reached something as near unanimity of viewpoint as is possible when economists seek practical remedies for society's ills.

That viewpoint can be briefly stated. A great loss of national income had taken place. It had hit some sections more than others and primary producers had suffered most of all. Some groups, especially wage-earners who were still at work and the receivers of fixed-interest incomes, had not felt the impact seriously; their receipts had actually gone up in value, because they now bought more goods. But those receipts imposed a heavy burden of costs on producers who were selling at falling prices, and the result would be disastrous to all in the long run.

To ease the burden where it pressed most, to redistribute the loss, and to reduce costs were essential parts of relief and prerequisites of recovery. How could this be done? The air was thick with conflict between the plans of deflationists and inflationists. The former belonged to the axe and tax school; their program was "Stick to sterling,[3] let prices follow the trend of gold. prices, balance budgets by reducing expenses and raising taxes, cut the coat according to the cloth." But since the cloth — the national income — shrunk one-third of its length in two years and the sterling value of exports fell nearly half, the cloth would be shrinking even as the tailor worked on it, and meanwhile its owner would die of starvation by dieting himself to the point where he could get into the garment. To drop metaphor, a full adjustment of public and private costs to the great and rapid fall in income would involve such a cutting of wages, dismissal of public servants, and pressure of taxation as could not be borne. Finally, the deflationists were silent on the question of fixed interest and other charges: these apparently were not to come down. Deflation of-

[3] As sterling was still on gold, this would have meant acceptance of gold prices.

fered no escape from depression; if recovery was to come that way, the patient would be killed in the process.

The inflationists had a more alluring song. They would restore the pre-depression price level by lowering the exchange value of the pound still further, by printing some notes, and by drastic changes in banking structure and practices. To the economists this plan was as bad and futile as was pure deflation. It might get out of hand if used to meet uncontrolled budget deficits, it would destroy confidence, and while it might raise prices it would raise the wrong prices, namely, general commodity prices rather than export prices. The burdened exporter would thus find his costs increased and be worse off than ever, or at best no better off.

If ruthless deflation and cheery inflation were alike ruled out, what should be done? Pursue a middle course, one which did not avoid deflation and inflation but took a little of each. Deflation was necessary to cut costs and redistribute loss more evenly; therefore wages, interest, rent, and public expenditure must be reduced, and reduced equally if possible, in order to give the public assurance that equality was being sought. Depreciation and inflation were necessary up to a certain point in order to cushion the exporters' income against the full drop in gold prices, help governments to finance limited deficits, and maintain prices and purchasing power.

This middle-course program gradually took shape during 1930. It was expounded in manifestos, memoranda, press articles, and lectures; it found in the reduction of real wages by the Arbitration Court a step toward deflation, and in the depreciation of the pound a desirable move in the other direction. The call of the premiers for a plan made possible the recommendation of several more steps.

The aim of the plan was to cope with a budget crisis marked by great deficits in the past year and greater ones looming ahead. Could the gap between income and revenue be narrowed, and how? Extra taxation might do something, but expenditure must be brought nearer to income rather than the reverse. A deflation of the cost of government was essential, and the only question to be answered was the extent to which this should be done.

The answer was found in the reduction of 20 per cent in money wages by the Arbitration Court. If private wage-earners had been deflated 20 per cent, let that figure be a general standard. Pensioners and public employees should take the same cut, and all expenditures capable of being reduced should suffer the same fate. But when all "adjustable expenditure" had been cut a fifth, there still remained a great deficit and a great load of "non-adjustable expenditure." This included interest, the cost of exchange on overseas payments, and unemployment relief; these three items accounted for two-fifths of the total public outgo.

But were all these items non-adjustable? Was there no way of reducing the interest load? On overseas bonds nothing could be done except by conversion and in 1931 conversion was impossible in London or New York. But half the debt—about £550,000,000, bearing 5¼ per cent—was held by Australians. If the interest on that amount could be reduced a great saving would be made. The bondholder might cry "breach of contract" if his interest was cut before the bond matured. But he had to recognize that in a crisis his bond's value rested on the solvency of the government that issued it. That government might pay him what was due and then take much of it from him in taxation; already there was a special tax of 7½ per cent on income from interest. It might inflate the currency and reduce the purchasing power of his interest. It might even default. If wage-earners had taken a cut, bondholders must do the same.

The economists therefore recommended a reduction of 15 per cent in interest on the internal public debt. The premiers combined this with the existing tax of 7½ per cent in a reduction of 22½ per cent. This step would reduce the interest rate to just over 4 per cent and save over £6,000,000. The necessary laws were passed, and bondholders were invited to do their bit by converting their holdings. The response was splendid, for 97 per cent of the debt was voluntarily converted; most of the remainder was compulsorily converted.

Public indebtedness was not the only fixed charge calling for attention. Bank rates, mortgage interest, and other fixed costs in private finance could scarcely be exempted from participation in the general deflation. The various states passed laws to reduce mortgage rates by 22½ per cent. Since most legislatures had already passed some form of moratorium legislation to restrict mortgagees from exercising their remedies against defaulters, the primary producer was both protected and relieved. By agreement among the banks, rates on deposits and advances were reduced one per cent, but the reduction applied only to new business, not to existing contracts.

Parity of sacrifice was more easily sought than found. Wages were not reduced equally at one stroke, and the lowering of living standards was uneven and patchy. The bank reductions still left some rates high, and the banks were called extortioners. Nevertheless the Premiers' Plan was a tonic, for it seemed to be a resolute way of facing crisis, it "created confidence in the capacity of the governments to make necessary adjustments," [4] and was as fair as possible in distributing the burden. The effort to bring deficits within manageable dimensions was valiant. Though it did not attain its objective immediately, because of deepening depression, the deficits of 1931–1932 were less than half the size they would have been without the plan. Next year a further effort was made, and was favored by the beginnings of recovery and of rising prices. The federal government ended the year with a surplus, although it had reduced some taxes and given an export bounty to grain-growers; and the states emerged less out of pocket than they had expected. The plan for 1933–1934 involved further tax reduction, a balanced budget for the Commonwealth, and a smaller deficit for the states. The Commonwealth ended with a surplus and the states drew a little nearer solvency. The plan for 1934–1935 seeks still better results.

This stalwart attempt to check the drift in public finance restored Australia's credit rating abroad, while the expansion of exports, combined with the decline in imports, restored the country's capacity to meet its external debts. Reward came in ability to convert part of

[4] D. B. Copland, "The Premiers' Plan in Australia," *International Affairs*, 13:88.

the overseas debt. Since October, 1932, £110,000,000 of bonds – about a quarter of the total – have been converted from an average rate of over 5½ per cent to one of 3¾ per cent. The saving in interest and exchange costs is over £2,000,000 yearly.

Steps taken to reduce public and private costs were all deflationary: they were acts which reduced incomes below the former level. But the Australian plan walked on two feet, and if one was on the deflation side of the road the other was on the inflation side. If we take Professor Copland's definition, inflationary action is that "which helps to sustain money incomes above the level they would tend to reach under the operation of a policy of adherence to an international gold standard"; [5] such action, for specific purposes and to a controlled amount, was just as important as efforts at "constructive deflation."

The purpose of inflation was twofold. In the first place it must minimize the fall in national income caused by the deflation of gold prices outside and counteract the deflationary actions on wages, interest, and government expenditure within the country. Australia could do little to prevent the fall in the price of its exports; but by depreciating its currency through exchange policy it could reduce the extent of the fall in terms of Australian pounds. The economists argued that "internal stability of the price level at the expense of external depreciation of the currency" was the desired goal of monetary policy.

In the second place, inflation must maintain to some

[5] Copland, *Australia in the World Crisis*, p. 116.

measured extent the purchasing power inside the country by bridging the gap between public revenue and curtailed public expenditure. If governments could spend only what they raised in taxes their activities must be curtailed to a cruel degree, and their spending of what they collected would only replace that of the people from whom the money had been taken. Their revenue must be supplemented by loans, obtained from the banks through the sale of treasury bills. This was no new practice, and as we have seen it had been checked by an ultimatum in 1931. But when the governments had bound themselves to budget reform and limited deficits some of the reluctance to lend vanished, and the floating debt of short-term treasury bills rose from twenty to fifty million pounds in a year and a half.

This was made possible by the expansion of credit by the Commonwealth Bank, and Professor Copland suggests that this expansion may have been as much as 65 per cent between the onset of the depression and 1933. This in turn had its effect at many points, the total result of which was maintained or increased purchasing power.

Professor Mills described the situation as follows: "Governments were pleased to be able to borrow in order to meet their ordinary requirements and for purposes of public works. Trading banks welcomed treasury bills as a method of investing idle resources which was both liquid and interest-bearing. The general public, in so far as they were aware of the process, felt that government expenditure was enabling the spending power of the community to be maintained. Australian economists considered them a safe method of inflation, because budget deficits were controlled, and preferable to the alternative of progressive deflation." [6]

The method of meeting treasury deficits by treasury bill loans and of propping up export prices by depreciating the currency had its dangers, but in 1931–1932 every country had to take risks and hope for the best. The currency depreciation was so modest in its scale that it failed to counteract the whole effect of falling prices outside; it was controlled and can be reduced or canceled if need be. What might have happened to inflation if the governments had not been able to keep their promise to control expenditure and reduce deficits we need not stop to consider, since policy and the beginning of recovery helped them to keep the promise. In the opinion of some Australians the time is now ripe for a reduction in the degree of currency depreciation, and since the early part of 1933 the amount of treasury bills outstanding has declined.

Australia's weathering of the storm was thus a mixture of orthodox and heterodox seamanship. She had her brain trust nearly two years before the term was coined in America; she tackled the necessary deflation with greater courage, skill, and rough justice than did any other country, and reached a realistic currency and credit policy more quickly than did most lands. In the Arbitration Court, the Loan Council, and the Commonwealth Bank she found that instruments fashioned in calmer days were now of great value. Her banking structure, with its few large banks and swarm of branches, had been well

[6] R. C. Mills, "The Lesson of Australia," *Index* (Stockholm), July, 1934, p. 156.

and cautiously managed and was therefore able to take the strain without cracking.

Her cattle and sheep men were inured to hard times, whether drought or depression, and the banks and wool-brokers had long ago learned the wisdom of carrying the pastoralist through the lean years, confident that when better days came the stricken would regain their strength and repay. Even in the worst days, when wool that cost 14d. to produce was selling at 8d., the sheep man was cared for by his financial agents as well as by a depreciated pound. He responded by selling whatever clip he had at whatever price he could get, instead of holding it back and thus piling up a great carry-over to weaken the market. He maintained production and even increased it in spite of prices that were low and unprofitable, and good seasons helped him. When therefore in 1933 wool prices began to recover rapidly, and jumped from 8d. to 14d., a people that had learned to exist on eightpence could now begin to hope that God was once more remembering his own country.

Rising wool prices came to cheer a country that was already taking heart. It had already virtually solved its external debt problem by reducing imports enormously while managing to maintain the value of its exports at the level to which they had fallen in the early stages of the depression. Its credits overseas were more than sufficient to meet its debits by 1931–1932. Given this condition and a balanced federal budget, prohibitions on imports could then be removed, some tariff rates cut, some federal taxes lowered. The interest on treasury bills began to fall, the price of stocks began to rise even in late

1931, and unemployment declined after the middle of 1932. Wholesale, retail, and export prices, which had remained comparatively stable from the beginning of 1931 to the latter part of 1932, suffered in sympathy with the American deflation of late 1932, but rose thereafter in sympathy with the world price recovery. These tokens of modest recovery were all evident in Australia long before they appeared in America, and some of them were apparent in the Antipodes earlier than in Britain. Few will question Professor Copland's confident claim that the basis of this recovery was laid in the Premiers' Plan and in the monetary policy pursued since early 1931.

Recovery came to a country that had paid the price in advance. The price demanded had not been prohibitive, for as Professor Mills says, "the policy adopted has always taken into account what people could stand, even in times of depression," and the genuine attempt to spread the sacrifice as fairly as possible established the belief that no one was getting a free ticket and no one was being charged too much.

National characteristics and political traits contributed something to the country's ability to pursue a set course. Australia has a small concentrated population, homogeneous in national origin and temper, rich in political tradition and experience, accustomed to discussing programs rather than personalities, ready to experiment, and with no exaggerated respect for individualism in economic affairs. Between the solid ranks of Labor and the right wing of big business is a section of salary-earners, farmers, and middle class which has a stake in the country in the form of large savings bank deposits, houses, and land.

That section is the balance wheel of public life, or, to change the metaphor, it swings the pendulum. Political power goes now to Labor, now to its opponents, as this floating vote condemns the stupidities or incompetence of the one or the extravagant, predatory plans of the other. The depression has seen instances in Australia, and to some extent in England in 1931, where the advocates of easy escapes and free painless dentistry, of inflation and of undiminished spending, of plundering the rich for the benefit of the rest, have been cast aside. In September, 1934, a federal government which had borne much of the burden and heat of the day was returned for a second term. Its opponents had promised to take the Commonwealth Bank under political control and make money available more abundantly at low rates of interest; some of them had promised oceans of free credit with which to provide income for old folks, invalids, widows, pensioners, unemployed, and ample funds for public works. Victory over such seductive adversaries seemed impossible to many well-informed onlookers, yet it came; the electorate approved what had been done for it and to it, and declined to follow the will o' the wisps.

One of the outstanding features of the Australian story is the service rendered by those three "institutions of national economic administration," the Loan Council, the Arbitration Court, and the Commonwealth Bank. Established in happier days, no one could have foreseen the part they were to play in stormy weather. They were

all political creations; the Council rested on an amendment of the constitution, the other two on federal stat-
utes. The Court and the Bank have been bitterly opposed
by some at their birth and during their career, and the
establishment of the Loan Council would probably have
been very difficult if the states had not thought they
were getting something for nothing by being allowed to
transfer their debts to the Commonwealth and by getting aid from the federal coffers in paying their interest
bills.

In erecting these three institutions Australia built more
wisely than she realized. The Loan Council could apply
the brake to uncontrolled spending and borrowing, the
Commonwealth Bank could force the Council to use
the brake, and the Court could lead the way in orderly
deflation. All three tasks were unpopular, and legislatures would have been loath to undertake them. It was
fortunate that they could be done by bodies which were
not exposed to the immediate control of the lawmakers
and were able to pursue an independent and courageous
course.

Their authority was nation-wide in its scope, and was
thus part of that trend toward the growth of the power
of central governments which has characterized the depression history of all federal countries. The trend was
visible long before depression came, and the struggle between the guardians of state rights and the advocates of
unification was at times fierce. In the opinion of Australian onlookers the movement toward centralization of
control is inevitable and will continue as part of the
country's adjustment to changing events. In the words

of Professor Portus, "Australia, and the world, may be forced to adopt some system of planned economy. This would necessitate considerable limitations on the freedom of enterprise, and such limitations themselves would need to be co-ordinated. The transition from an uncontrolled to a planned economy in any federal system would certainly be accompanied by a gradual increase in the power of central governments. Only strong governments can plan." [7]

These words were written in Sydney, not in Columbia University.

[7] G. V. Portus, *Australia, an Economic Interpretation* (1933), pp. 98–99.

CHAPTER EIGHT

CANADA MUDDLES THROUGH

THE HEADLINES OF CANADIAN NEWSPAPERS AND THE
tables of the Dominion Bureau of Statistics have for
many months past told a tale of recovery. In Canada, as
in the United States, the darkest hour came in the winter
of 1932–1933, but was not so black as next door, for the
solidity of the banking system spared the country a
banking crisis, and outside the prairie wheat belt the depression was probably less severe than in the United
States.

An index number of the "physical volume of business" rose from 68 in March, 1933, to 99.6 in May, 1934,
and was thus almost back to the monthly average of
1926, which is the base for the index. Many of the detailed indices which are merged to make this composite
photograph were not yet back to the level of 1926, but
some of them had gone far beyond it. The figure for industrial production has recovered over half the distance
it lost between 1929 and 1933, and the volume of employment is now four-fifths that of 1929. The number
of persons on relief lists has fallen from the peak of
1,360,000, or one-eighth of the population, but was still
nearly a million in the summer of 1934. In Ontario,
the most heavily populated and industrialized province,
one-seventh of the people were on those lists in April,
1933, but the fraction was only one-twelfth in mid-

1934. The price of wheat, the value of foreign trade, the output of minerals, all have recovered much ground, but have still far to travel.

If you ask a Canadian what the country has done to cause such welcome developments, his reply is nearly always, "Nothing." If you jog his memory he will recall that the tariff was raised quite early in the depression, that 1930 and 1932 were full of talk about salvation by Empire trade bargains, that relief of the unemployed and of prairie farmers has absorbed a lot of effort and money, that taxes have been raised high, and that recently a certain constructive liveliness on the dominion political front has produced a central bank, a marketing scheme, a mild inflation of the note issue, and elaborate relief plans for debtor farmers. But of a plan comparable to Australia's, a deal like America's, or a commercial, financial, and fiscal re-shuffle like Britain's, Canada has had nothing.

In part this quiescence may be due to the personality and political outlook of those who have controlled Canadian affairs since 1930. It may be explained to some extent by defects or gaps in the political equipment of the country, for Canada had nothing comparable to the Loan Council, the Commonwealth Bank, or the Arbitration Court of Australia, and the obstacles in the path of a dominion extension of power over the provinces are constitutionally great. But most stress must be placed on the fact that the nature of Canada's economy made it difficult for her to do much to dispel depression. She had to adopt a stoic attitude and wait till improvements outside her borders brought an end to hard times.

That economy rested on the exploitation and export of primary products to the great industrial consuming communities of Europe and the United States and to other smaller areas which lacked the particular natural resources that Canada had in abundance. Her economic history began with two F's — fur and fish; then it added two more — forest and farm. Toward the end of the nineteenth century, a fifth F was added — the factory, to supply the needs of an expanding population, to equip the westward movement, and to take advantage of imperial preference. At the same time large areas that were unfit for settlement became valuable. On them was the lumber needed by the builder and the paper-maker, and the falling water that could be harnessed to provide electricity. Under them were deposits which have made Canada one of the world's largest and most varied mineral producers. In 1929 her output was worth more than $300,000,000, and mounting rapidly. She led the world in the production of asbestos and supplied it with four-fifths of the nickel it was needing in greater quantities for its alloys. She was climbing to second place, or had already reached it, in the mining of gold, cobalt, and zinc, stood third in copper production, and fourth in lead and silver.

Given such rich and varied resources, Canada's growth after 1900 was rapid, first as prairie producer of wheat and then as miner and pulp- or paper-maker. Between 1900 and 1928 her population nearly doubled; the volume of her exports grew probably fourfold and the value eightfold. About one-third of her goods went abroad; in 1929 she ranked fifth among the world's external traders, but in the value of trade per head of population she ran Denmark a close race for second place.

Her expansion was tied up most intimately with the United States and Great Britain, by three strong strands — exports, imports, and capital supply. These countries were her best markets, and although minor purchasers were growing in relative importance, two-thirds of her exports in 1929 went to the two big customers. Britain took just under a third of them, especially foods and some metal. The United States took over a third, and was the chief market for the paper, pulp, lumber, nickel, copper, asbestos, silver, furs, and whisky. The farmer looked across the Atlantic for his market, the miner and forest worker looked south. If these two customers were stricken, closed their doors, or could not buy, there was little that Canada could do but wait till they recovered and came back to market.

Great Britain and the United States were also Canada's chief sources of supply of goods and capital. More than two-thirds of Canada's imports came from the United States, and Britain was a poor second. Britain had been the first source of capital supply, and contributed chiefly to public needs and railroads; but New York became important after 1914, and supplied funds for governments, for manufactures, mining, and the paper industry. By 1929 nearly six billion dollars of capital had come into the country, in the rough proportion of five from the south to three from London.

A large part of those six billion dollars and much Canadian capital besides had been sunk in costly equipment for production and transportation. To get the wheat of the prairies to the coast, vast outlays had been made on canals, railroads, and elevators. The Canadian government had spent heavily to make a better water channel from the head of the Lakes to Montreal; it had thrown a railroad across the wastes of northeastern Manitoba to carry grain to Hudson's Bay; it had built other lines or encouraged private enterprise to build them in order to give additional links between the prairies and the coasts. Large public or private investments of native and imported capital had gone to provide costly plant for hydro-electric generation, mining, and the pulp and paper industry.

To carry this load of capital charges and external debt, Canada had to rely chiefly on the volume and value of her wheat exports and on the sale of her other products to the United States. She paid her interest bills out of an excess of exports, out of new borrowings, out of income received on Canadian money invested abroad, and by entertaining American tourists. But if the wheat output was hit by bad seasons, if grain prices fell seriously, if the American boom demand for metals and paper fell, or the tourist traffic dropped off, her domestic situation and her ability to meet her external obligations would be seriously injured. She would be left with an expensive public and private plant for production and transportation, but with a shrunken income out of which to pay the fixed charges on public or corporation bonds, to defray the operating costs of government, and to live.

The collapse of farm prices and of the American boom therefore hit Canada twice. Fortunately there was no such drastic stoppage of external loans as in Australia. In 1930 these were larger than in any other post-war year, and they helped to ease the strain caused by the rapid shift from a large excess of exports to one of imports. But this consolation was slight in face of the fall in the return from exports from nearly $1,400,000,000 in the last boom year to less than $500,000,000 in the deepest year of depression. By 1931 the statisticians estimated that the net value of the country's total production had fallen a third, and the prairie provinces declared that their gross income from agriculture had fallen two-thirds by 1932.

Canada's depression problems and her attempts to cope with them have had no peculiar features. There was the farmer trying to bear a load of debt and taxes, and to buy manufactured goods that had fallen 23 per cent in price, with farm products that had dropped 62 per cent. There was the army of unemployed wage-earners, and of stockholders whose shares paid no return and whose company was headed for the rocks of receivership. There were ten governments trying to meet incessant demands for aid, pay interest bills, and provide work or relief out of shrinking revenue; and in the case of the dominion government there was an acute railroad problem as well.

The farmer's plight was the most serious, for three-tenths of the "gainfully employed" population worked on the land. On the diversified farms east of Lake Huron varied production provided sustenance at least, and there were near-by urban markets. But in parts of the prairies one-crop farming prevailed and was often the only possible sort. There the collapse of wheat prices,[1] coupled with drought and grasshoppers, spelled disaster not merely to the individual farmer but to the earnings of the equipment that handled his crops, and to the political and social structure of regions that had only one source of income. Saskatchewan was the chief sufferer; her plight resembled that of similarly situated states south of the border, of such wheat and wool states as South Australia, and of such industrial one-crop areas as we saw in Lancashire and Durham. Local governments defaulted on their bonds as farmers failed to pay taxes; the struggle to keep the schools open was only partly successful; the doctor and storekeeper could collect no money, savings bank funds shriveled up, and the commercial banks had to stop supplying farm credit.

To prop up this crumbling rural fabric, provincial and dominion governments gave a hand. A bonus on wheat was paid for a time. The banks were guaranteed against loss on advances made to the provincial cooperative wheat pools. Those pools had been the West's attempt at "orderly marketing," but their work was shot to pieces in 1929–1930, and for their preservation public aid was essential. To stabilize the wheat market, the dominion government guaranteed the banks against loss in financing hedging operations by the cooperative agency; finally it put one man in charge and supplied him with funds. But most efforts to "put a bottom in the market" were unavailing if they were made before the market found its own bottom.

[1] In July, 1929, No. 1 Northern wheat was quoted in store at Fort William at $1.79 a bushel. In December, 1932, the price was 39 cents.

The only cure for the prairies was a rising price. When it came in 1933 it was the result of movements in sterling and the dollar, and "may be generally attributed to the monetary policy of Great Britain and the United States" [2] rather than to any action taken by Canada, just as that of 1934 has been due to drought. In the interest of higher prices Canada fought valiantly at the World Economic Conference in 1933 for agreement on reduction of wheat acreage and export. She had some success, in the pacts to limit exports during the next two years. In the United States, promises of money compensation failed to secure the full desired reduction in acreage, and in Canada there was no offer of compensation and no planned reduction of acreage, but only one of export. The drought of 1934 may relieve the situation, and convert the large surplus from a liability to an asset.

For the debt-laden farmer relief acts were passed by the provincial legislatures, restraining creditors or providing for the revision of contracts. In this salvage work the dominion government took a hand in 1934, by providing simple, cheap, and quick methods for bankruptcy proceedings or for revising contracts by agreement between debtor and creditor. This law has only just come into operation, and the degree to which it will be used and abused cannot be anticipated.

One outcome of the agricultural depression has been the provision for controlled marketing. The plans are largely based on ideas drawn from the United States and from the methods of Elliotism in Great Britain. Ontario

[2] H. A. Innis, "Economic Recovery in Canada in 1933," *Commerce Journal* (Toronto), February, 1934, p. 4.

in 1934 passed the Milk Control Act, and the dominion legislature followed with the Natural Products Marketing Act. Its aim is "to improve the methods and practices of marketing of natural products." It can be applied to products of animal, vegetable, forest, and marine origin, and to foods and drinks made from them. Boards may be set up, dissentient minorities must obey, and all producers must be licensed. The quality and quantity of goods sent to market are to be controlled, levies will be made, and producers may be compensated for loss incurred if their goods are withheld from sale or are sold in a market where the currency is depreciated.

The Ontario act is now in operation, and the dominion law is receiving its trial run in the apple export trade. By regulating the dispatch of some two million barrels of fruit, oversupplies and shortages of Canadian produce in the British market are to be avoided, better grading will be possible, and higher prices obtained. How far control will spread in the domestic and export trade depends on the success of these two experiments, and on the extent to which the British policy of restricted imports is developed. Controlled exports will be the corollary of measured imports.

For coping with heavy protracted unemployment Canada was about as well equipped as the United States. She had an unemployment service which helped to bring idle men in contact with jobs; but she had no unemployment insurance, and the organization of relief, a duty that fell on the shoulders of the municipalities and of philanthropic groups, was weak. When the present dominion government took office in 1930 its leader, Mr.

Bennett, had made unqualified promises to provide work, not doles. His party would "find work for all who are willing to work, or perish in the attempt." The jobs would come partly by taking them from "workmen in other lands," for a policy of "Canada First" meant higher protection; but they would spring also from "national undertakings which will give work to our workmen" on important necessary public works.

In 1930 the problem looked small and simple. Dominion, provincial, and municipal governments turned to public works and to relief, with the emphasis on the former. But the cost of public works was heavy, the impression on the unemployment figures was small, and some of the works were neither important nor necessary. By the end of 1932 the total public works bill was mounting toward $200,000,000, while direct relief had cost only $23,000,000. The job-makers therefore decided to transfer their interest to direct relief, which might degrade the idle but was cheaper. Public works still continued on a small scale, but revived rapidly when a cabinet was drawing near to election time; and in 1934 the dominion government decided to inflate the note issue by $40,000,000 for a program of public works. Land colonization also received some attention; the result has been a mere drop in the bucket, yet Quebec is still making earnest efforts to put men on the land.

Direct relief was cheaper, but still unsatisfactory and costly enough. For every dollar raised by a municipality the province added another dollar and the Dominion decided to help by contributing a third. Some municipalities were so burdened that they could not find enough money, and the contribution of the larger governments must be increased. In a Montreal newspaper of July 25, 1934, the lucid headline appeared, "Dole continuance impossible minus new revenue taps," which, being interpreted, meant that some Quebec local authorities could not maintain relief payments unless they were allowed to levy new or heavier taxes.

While the municipalities asked for more, provincial and dominion treasurers grew alarmed at the size of the sums they had to provide, and uneasy over the administration of relief. The more stricken provinces were hard put to raise funds for any purpose, and had to borrow money from the federal government in order to hand it on to the local authorities. Further, there was a suspicion that mayors and other officials were more generous and less careful when the bulk of the cost of relief was being met by outside funds. There seems to have been much ground for this suspicion.

In July, 1934, Ottawa said that conditions had improved so much that it intended to stop its contribution of a third, and would give only a fixed sum far below that paid out in earlier years. It had its own pressing needs; it had been forced by circumstances into the relief field as Washington was, and had poured a great sum of money onto the thirsty land. It was glad to get out of its emergency obligation as soon as circumstances gave a justification or pretext.

The transfer of jobs from "workmen in other lands" was sought by a very vigorous policy of higher protection. Duties were raised; to *ad valorem* duties specific rates were added, based on weight, area, or volume rather than on value. Customs officials made arbitrary valuations, not merely of goods coming from lands with depreciated currencies but also from the United States. There were primage duties, sales taxes, dumping duties; and those Britons who thought a depreciated pound would help them to gain easier access to the Canadian customer soon found the advantage more than swept away when, after a long series of calculations and special imposts, they learned what duty must be paid. British shoemakers, for instance, saw their exports to Canada fall from 750,000 pairs in 1929 to 106,000 in 1933. These obstacles helped to check importation, and the value of goods entering the country fell so rapidly that in 1932 the country once more had an excess of exports, in spite of a fall of two-thirds in the value of exports. But the shrinkage of capital imports was probably as important as the tariff; and employment continued to decline.

"Canada First" did not conflict with "Empire Second," and Mr. Bennett led the onslaught on Britain's free trade stubbornness at the Imperial Conference in London in 1930. That attack was in vain, and some of the overseas premiers made little effort to conceal their chagrin or their hope that soon a more sensible government would occupy Downing Street. Their hopes were fulfilled in 1931, and the Ottawa agreements followed in 1932. From those Canada could gain much; the varied character of her primary products and of her manufacturing industries, the lack of domestic supplies of many of these goods in Great Britain and most of the dominions, and the preferences all combined to make the imperial market more valuable to Canada.

One result — perhaps a temporary one — of the depression and of the incipient recovery has been to change the relative importance of Great Britain and the United States as markets for Canadian products.[3] If some things attracted more trade to Britain, others checked the flow southward. The Hawley-Smoot tariff, the prohibitive duties imposed on copper and lumber in 1932, the general decline of American production and of demand for lumber, paper, and metals, and the weakening of the American dollar in terms of its northern neighbor, all tended to reduce the American demand for Canadian produce. The shrinkage in the area of advertisements in American newspapers and periodicals lengthened the life of many a Canadian tree. In 1933 Britain took a bigger portion of Canada's exports of the goods she had always bought; the United States bought a smaller part of the goods that went chiefly to her; and of goods that found markets in both countries the British share jumped while the American fell. Some of these trends will probably be checked with the recovery of American demand; but the imperial market has become proportionately much more important to the Canadian producer.

Depression bore heavily on Canadian public finances, and relief is only just coming in sight. For thirty years the accumulation of public debt had gone on merrily; the total liability of all public bodies in 1929 stood at $740 per head of the population, and had almost doubled in a decade. It was not all dead weight, though a slice of it was war debt. Against it were assets in the form of

[3] See an article on this subject by J. D. Gibson in the *Canadian Bankers Journal*, April, 1934.

transportation facilities and other publicly owned utilities; but some of these were quickly reduced by the depression to a point where they contributed little or nothing toward meeting the fixed debt charges incurred for their construction and might even fail to earn their operating costs; and much debt was neither directly nor indirectly productive of revenue. A large part of the public outgo was rigid, non-adjustable, and must be met no matter what happened to revenue.

The balancing of depression budgets was impossible, and additional debt had to be incurred to meet deficits and pay relief or public works costs. The lack of any equivalent to a Loan Council that would limit borrowing, control treasurers, and put the national credit behind provincial debts, exposed the more unfortunate provinces to much higher interest rates than could be secured by the "better risks." For instance, Quebec raised a loan at about 3 per cent in 1934, while stricken Saskatchewan had to pay 5¼ per cent. The dominion government in 1933 told the provinces they would get no further financial aid unless they balanced their budgets or kept their deficits within bounds. If they failed to do so, it threatened them with the overlordship of a financial controller. It has had to come to the aid of the four western provinces, and has lent $60,000,000 of its own borrowings to them; it has thereby accepted responsibility to creditors for the interest and principal, yet on the latest loans made to two of these provinces the interest rate is 5 per cent.

While deficits and new borrowings were general, Canada could benefit little and slowly from that reduction of interest rates which eased the Australian situation and lowered the cost of public and of private loans in Britain. In May, 1933, the banks reduced interest rates on deposits one-half per cent, and passed this on to public borrowers. But it did nothing to the existing bonded debt. Some of this was held abroad, some by Canadians.[4] An appeal to the latter to convert their holdings before they matured was regarded as impracticable by the government, and investment dealers cried out that contracts must be honored. Conversion could take place only when the day of maturity dawned. Not till late 1933 did a large internal loan mature and permit conversion to a lower rate. By 1937 this procedure will have given relief on a quarter of the dominion bonds, and on only a third of those held in the country. Substantial relief for the Dominion is still far off, and even farther off for the provinces and municipalities.

One great cause of Canada's financial worries is its railroad problem. Ten million people live in four areas, separated by geographical barriers but linked together and to the oceans by two great railroads. One, the Canadian Pacific, is a private enterprise, lavishly helped in its infancy by grants of land and money, and profitably operated for decades prior to the present one. The other, the Canadian National, is publicly owned. Its origin was a jumble of high and low politics and finance, of boom-time optimism, and of extravagant hopes inspired by prairie expansion. The Dominion built some lines and was creditor or guarantor of others; when the others,

[4] Of the dominion debt three-fourths was payable in Canada, 11 per cent in New York, and 11.5 per cent in London.

victims of squandermania, fell into its hands in 1917 it had 22,000 miles of track and a mountain of bonded debt incurred in their construction. To weld the lines into an efficient railroad system was possible; to earn enough to meet operating and debt charges was not, even in the best years. The public purse was raided to pay some of the interest, and the national debt was increased to provide new capital for improvement and expansion. When earnings collapsed money had to be borrowed to pay part of the operating expenses as well. In 1933 the railroad was costing the country a million dollars a week, while the debt on it was approaching three billion dollars and mounting every day.

This railroad situation is probably the biggest and most difficult problem confronting Canada today. The line is wrecking the finances of its owner and ravaging those of its rival, the C. P. R. A royal commission which examined the matter in 1931–1932 shied away from all thought of amalgamation of the two lines, since that would create a monopoly, make the system unwieldy, and be unsuitable for more prosperous times. It recommended that the identity of the lines be maintained, but that they cooperate wherever possible. Cooperation and competition may seem incompatible, and the savings due to cooperation have been small as yet. Salvation might come through a great reduction of interest charges, which seems financially impossible; from amalgamation, which seems politically unlikely; or through a vast expansion of traffic, which is improbable since the day of expanding prairie settlement and production has apparently ended. Every country has its dead-weight debt, the price of war or of excessive optimism; Canada has to pay the price of both.

She has, however, been spared one acute financial problem. Though her corporation finances were chaotic, her banks escaped the crisis that swept the United States to the brink of the precipice. Her corporation history during the boom was like that of her neighbor. The thirst for amalgamations, holding companies, stock bonuses, no par stock, and other manifestations of the new era was only a little less intense in the cooler latitudes of Toronto and Montreal, and it was a Canadian magnate who preached the new gospel that insurance companies should buy common stock. The results were disastrous. The bursting of balloons filled the list of Canadian receiverships with the names of important corporations. Of the boom creations which survive, many "are today so overcapitalized that only by keeping wages and employment at a minimum can they ever hope to pay their common shareholders a decent return. The problem of corporate capital indebtedness is the twin of the problem of public indebtedness." [5] Neither of them is near solution.

The banks fared better. In all the years since 1867 only twenty-six banks have failed; the last one closed its doors in 1923. The causes of this strength are found in banking law, structure, and practice. Banking is subject to one law only, that of the Dominion. That law is reexamined every decade and is amended in the light of experience and new needs. The establishment of a new bank is not easy; of its minimum nominal capital of $500,000, two-fifths must be on hand within two years.

[5] *Toronto Daily Star*, June 25, 1934.

Its stockholders must accept double liability for twice the amount of their holdings. Detailed monthly statements must be sent to the government, and public inspection is strict. Banks must not lend on real estate or do trust business. They cannot lend money to bank officers or buy bank stock. They can issue notes up to the limit of their share capital plus the amount of their deposits of gold and dominion notes in a central gold reserve. They need not keep any specific or minimum cash reserve. In short, the law alternates restriction and freedom in the light of experience.

Structure and practice are as important as the law. By a process of amalgamation the number of banks has fallen from thirty-eight in 1900 to ten today. By a policy of establishing branches these ten banks have over three thousand outposts. One of them has 738 branches spread from the Maritime Provinces to the Pacific; another, with head offices in Montreal, has 560, of which nearly 200 are west of Lake Superior and 2 are in the Yukon. As the West grew the branch bank came to serve it. Behind it was the strength and strict control of the East, and in hard times the rates on loans made to Canadian prairie dwellers were lower than those in adjacent American states. A nation-wide bank could diversify its assets, instead of putting them all into one area or industry; it was big enough to build up large reserves, to pay for competent management, and to make money by sticking to its main job, commercial banking, instead of having to stray into other fields and take greater risks.

Even in small towns there was usually rivalry between branches of two banks. This did not affect interest rates, for agreements kept them uniform as well as stable in good times and bad. But in other respects there was room for competition in commercial banking, in financing the moving of the crops, in dealing in foreign exchange, in providing "a line of credit" for borrowers, in buying and selling securities, and in underwriting bonds.

As commercial banks these institutions have served their depositors, borrowers, and stockholders well. In humdrum days of gold standards, active foreign trade, and stable exchange rates, their facilities, supplemented by some governmental aid, and by a few exchange dealers, sufficed to meet the country's needs. The Dominion Department of Finance issued notes which originally had been heavily backed by gold; but during and after the war the gold support grew more slender. In addition the department could issue notes without a gold backing, and lend them to banks on the security of Canadian, British, or American bonds or treasury bills, or of promissory notes or bills of exchange which were based on title to commodities or drawn for industrial, agricultural, or commercial purposes.

The currency and credit system was in this way given a degree of elasticity. The banks paid interest on these notes, and by adding them to their cash reserves they were able to make new loans to the extent of eight or ten times the amount added. The dominion note issue influenced the capacity of the banks to lend and of the public to borrow and buy. Meanwhile the country's gold supply rose or fell according to surpluses or deficits in the balance of international payments, and the Canadian dollar was kept near par.

When depression came and gold standards fell, it was not sufficient to be a good routine banker in Moose Jaw, Medicine Hat, or Montreal, and finance ministers must know the answers to new questions. What, for example, was to happen to the exchange value of the dollar? While Britain and the United States were on gold, Canada must remain so, though nominally she went off it, restricted export of gold except under license, and bought the output of her gold mines.

In that decision she was largely influenced by the views of her bankers and by the need for servicing her external debts. The bankers said that banking policy in a debtor country could not "safely undertake to influence the movement of domestic commodity prices whether or not our dollar is stabilized in relation to the currencies of the great creditor countries." [6] Internal price stability could not be secured by exchange policy. The debt payments called for a dollar at full value abroad. Australia sacrificed exchange parity for internal price stability; Canada did the opposite. The size of her external obligations was large, and was estimated by Mr. Bennett as costing a million dollars a day, of which roughly three-quarters was due in New York. As long- and short-term loans were still necessary to meet deficits, the dollar must be kept up if possible, by borrowing to pay interest bills, by exporting gold, by restricting imports, and by any other method that was within reach.

In spite of these efforts the Canadian dollar was unable

[6] Evidence of the general manager of the Bank of Montreal before the Macmillan royal commission on Canadian banking and currency, 1933.

to stand the blow given by Britain's departure from gold. That action sent sterling down to a discount of one-third in Montreal, but the repercussion helped to depress the Canadian dollar nearly a fifth in New York. The fall of sterling made some Canadian goods dearer in England and therefore reduced their sale; the recovery of sterling in 1933 repaired that damage. The fall of Canadian dollars in America made Canadian goods cheaper there, but added to the cost of debt service: the recovery in 1933–1934 made goods dearer again.

Tied to two external currencies instead of one, Canada felt the effect of exchange fluctuations more severely than Australia, and had no institution capable of handling the situation. The service of the banks was good so far as it went, but something more was needed to fit the banks into a financial system that would be more than an efficient servant of commerce. This view was endorsed by a majority of the members of the royal commission which examined the Canadian banking scene in 1933. A banking system must "bear a share in trying to maintain stability and to regulate the quantity and flow of credit; it must interest itself in price levels, in the fluctuations of exchange, in international monetary cooperation – in short, in all the matters which concern national finance." That was the job of a central bank; it could not be done by ten commercial banks and a finance department with many other demands upon their attention.

The banking community in general opposed this verdict, but the Bank of Canada was nevertheless set up by parliament in 1934. Its function is "to regulate credit and currency in the best interests of the economic life of the nation; to control and protect the external value of the national monetary unit and to mitigate by its influence internal fluctuations in the general level of production, trade, prices, and employment, so far as may be possible within the scope of monetary action" — a powerful saving clause. It will rediscount bills and buy securities in order to get more funds into the hands of the banks, and its rediscount rate will rise or fall as it thinks constraint or stimulus is needed. It will engage in "open market operations," buying and selling bills and securities. It will gradually take over the note issue from the government and the banks, mobilize the gold reserve, look after the foreign exchange rate, and serve as financial aid and adviser to governments. It is privately owned, as are the Bank of England and the Federal Reserve system; but its profits are limited to a modest rate, and its managing officers, though chosen by the directors, must be approved by the government. Its first governor has just been appointed by the cabinet.

It comes into being in days of recovery, and its infancy will be pleasant if recovery continues. If it makes good, Canadians may wish it had been born ten years ago. They are already entertaining many such wishes. The depression has torn rents in their economic and social fabric; and institutions, ideas, and practices which passed unchallenged five years ago are now being raked with heavy fire.

For this belated wave of self-criticism and desire for reform, the New Deal is in part responsible. When President Roosevelt began to talk to a hundred and twenty million dispirited Americans, many of Canada's disheartened ten millions listened in. Their own leaders could, of course, declare with pride that some of his aims and methods were old in Canada. She had sound banks, she had gone to the aid of the grain-grower, had spent much on public works, and had some labor laws that ranked as advanced in North America. Or they could lament that a New Deal was impossible in Canada. If America cared to recover herself into bankruptcy, Canada could not afford it, since she was an exporter and debtor. Further, there were serious constitutional difficulties. Under the British North America Act the regulation of industrial conditions was a provincial prerogative, with which Ottawa could not interfere. To transfer control to dominion hands would require a constitutional amendment, and such amendment was not easily secured since the consent of all the provinces had to be obtained. Canada had better watch and wait.

Not all Canadians were satisfied to watch, wait, or play the Pharisee. Events and revelations suggested that perhaps Canada needed codes. An occasional strike uncovered sweated working conditions and workers who were supplementing starvation wages by securing public relief. A speech made in early 1934 by Mr. H. H. Stevens, minister for trade and customs, contained some criticism of marketing methods, and the sensation created thereby led to a parliamentary investigation into "price spreads and mass buying." The inquiry is not yet concluded, but the impression given by the evidence presented so far is that many producers of farm and factory products can sell only to giant processors, packers, or distributors. Many of these buyers developed megalomania during the boom, and now have to meet the cost of maintaining expensive plants or swollen capital structures. They use their great buying power to force the producer's prices down and thus drive him to reduce the wages of his workers. But the overhead costs of distribution necessitate a great spread between the price paid him and that charged to the consumer. The giant business units are not manifestations of the economies of large-scale operation, but of fantastic finance. If one penetrates behind their imposing façades, one finds men making shoes for ten cents an hour or five dollars a week, women making riding breeches at $1.15 a dozen and producing five pairs a day, or receiving thirty cents for making a dozen pairs of boys' pants, less five cents for thread.

The needle, shoe, and furniture industries were, as ever and in all countries, the centers of exploitation, and their labor was employed "on a basis that is a disgrace to Canada." But other producers had fared little better. "Outrageous and scandalous prices" had been paid to stock-raisers by a packing company which was enjoying record prosperity; "something like thirty million dollars had been gouged" out of the pulp and paper industries by the financial Pharaohs, leaving a healthy industry exhausted; tobacco, steel, department and chain stores, all were on the black list, and an "incomprehensible disregard for ethics [had] characterized some of the leaders of finance and industry." If America had its Pecora, Canada had its Stevens.[7]

[7] These statements are taken from the evidence and from the report of a private address given by Mr. Stevens in late July, 1934. Mimeographed copies of this address were distributed, and then mysteriously withdrawn.

The inquiry provoked much strong language. One cabinet minister said "further governmental control might prove necessary to prevent a small group of exploiters from wrecking the social life of Canada."[8] The mayor of Montreal announced that "revolution is at our doors" and could only be prevented if the government enforced business morality on business and finance.[9] At about the same time a dominion minister refused to approve a plan for the reorganization of the capital structure of a large corporation which had been inflated during the boom, on the ground that the proposals were "not equitable to one class of shareholders." In commenting on this novel action one financial editor wrote, "Had it been done in the last ten years the dose of poisonous financing that has helped to bring us to our present predicament might have been avoided."[10] The veto "encourages one to think that Rooseveltian ideas are creeping into the public life of Canada."

Those ideas have found favor in the eyes of many. Producers and merchants have suggested that codes might be good for their occupations, though their interest seems to be confined to the clauses restricting competition. Two Liberal governments which have recently been swept into office have taken or promised action to improve labor conditions. British Columbia in 1934 passed minimum wage acts and a law to regulate working hours. It set up a Board of Industrial Relations, which has limited hours of work in many occupations and fixed minimum wages for men, women, and young persons. In On-

[8] *Toronto Daily Star*, June 30, 1934.
[9] *Ibid.*, June 27, 1934.
[10] *Ibid.*, June 29, 1934.

tario a new cabinet has announced that codes to stamp out sweating will be rushed through the legislature when it meets. The burden of relief has driven many to see the need for unemployment insurance and for a national health insurance plan.

Five years in the Slough of Despond are thus producing much heart-searching. Some Liberals and Conservatives are saying strange things, while on the left flank an alliance of farmers, trade unionists, and urban middle class has stepped into the political arena, and has spent the last two years seeking to criticize and convert. For criticism it lacks no material; the domination of the country and of the old political parties by large industrial and financial interests is frankly admitted, and the transfer of natural resources from public to private hands has sprinkled Canadian political history with scandals. For conversion it paints a picture of a "cooperative commonwealth, in which the principle regulating production, distribution, and exchange will be the supplying of human needs and not the making of profits."

Its ultimate objective is "the establishment of a planned socialized economic order, in order to make possible the most efficient development of the national resources and the most equitable distribution of the national income." Its immediate proposals include the socialization of the country's banking and financial system; it seeks to protect the farmer from foreclosure, write down farm debts, establish an effective publicly owned rural credits system, and control the processing and marketing of farm produce; it urges a large-scale program of public works, especially a national housing scheme, national regulation of working conditions, a nation-wide plan of social insurance, and effective protection of workers' rights of bargaining through their own unions.[11]

This Cooperative Commonwealth Federation, this "alliance of proletariat, agrariat, and salariat," strives to achieve its objectives by winning political power. It has waged campaigns in provincial elections and won the votes of one-third the electors in British Columbia, of a quarter in Saskatchewan, and of a twelfth in Ontario; but it has won only a few seats in the legislatures. Its hope of securing political supremacy is remote, but its influence may be large enough to provoke the other parties to steal planks from its platform and take half steps where it proposes full ones.

Canada thus emerges from depression influenced by thunder to the south and by rumblings at home. As Professor Innis remarks, "In some sense this is Canada's first serious depression. . . . The cushion provided by virgin natural resources has for the first time shown signs of serious deflation,"[12] and the fall has been onto hard earth. After a term of exuberant expansion comes the need for creating order, imposing control, seeking security. That need has to be met partly by voluntary group action, partly by political action. For the former the farmers and the business world have shown they have some aptitude, but the wage-earner's ability to organize whether as producer or as consumer has been small. For political action an overhauling of the whole

[11] F. H. Underhill, "The C. C. F. Convention and After," *Canadian Forum*, September, 1934.
[12] H. A. Innis, "Economic Conditions in Canada, 1931–1932," *Economic Journal*, March, 1932, p. 15.

machinery of government seems necessary. In the words of a Canadian, "The truth is that we have outgrown the British North America Act. The Dominion of Canada is attempting today to carry on the highly complex life of a modern industrial state under a constitution drawn up for a primitive community, scarcely emerging from pioneer agricultural conditions." [13]

Worse still, the constitution of 1867 was an expression of the current doctrine of laissez faire. As an instrument for borrowing much money, for alienating natural resources, for encouraging industrial development, and for waging war the dominion constitution has proved adequate. But for the tasks of aid and control, especially in depressed days, it has been found wanting, and a thorough readjustment of the powers of the provinces and of the central government seems essential.

Meanwhile economic and political forces have been at work lifting parts of Canadian economic life out of the worst of their misfortunes. If wheat has moved upward slowly, the metal and forest industries have recovered more quickly. Falling prices and wages have reduced production costs, new plants constructed during the depression have come to production point, and ruthless weeding out of inefficient pulp and paper mills has reduced the excess productive capacity. External forces have played their part. The higher costs of production under the NRA favored Canadian firms in competition with American rivals in overseas areas. It is claimed, for instance, that exports of lumber from British Columbia have largely ousted American woods in many Pacific

[13] *Round Table*, September, 1934, p. 815.

markets. The building boom in Britain brought large orders to Canadian forests, and the recovery of sterling increased the purchases of Canadian produce.

Revival in the United States swelled the demand for pulp, paper, and metals. The depreciation of the American dollar eased the burden of interest payments in New York, while the enhancement in value of gold and silver was a gift to Canadian producers of those metals. The revival of tourist traffic made the chief traffic lanes busier, and growing activity in the lumber and metal industries stimulated the railroads a little.[14] The stricter regulation of the stock market in New York threatens to turn some habitués of Wall Street to Toronto or Montreal in search of a new stamping ground — a threat which may call for a new kind of immigration restriction.

If recovery continues, some of Canada's unsolved problems, such as debt adjustment and railroad finance, may shrink, solve themselves, or be shelved. If, under the fear of war or the pressure of economic nationalism, European countries continue to protect their grain-growers, the great prairie plant must face a decline, or at best a stabilization, of its export market, and a reduction of the acreage under wheat. How to adjust this reduction so that it will "occur in those areas least suited to the production of wheat calls for a further application of the principles of economic planning and of state control."[15] Laissez faire will be a poor commander, especially of forces in retreat.

[14] H. A. Innis, "Economic Recovery in Canada, 1933," *Commerce Journal*, February, 1934, pp. 4–10.
[15] D. A. MacGibbon, "The Wheat Problem," *University of Toronto Quarterly*, January, 1934, p. 244.

INDEX